Advance Praise for
Food Security for the Faint of Heart

If any book was ever published at the right moment this is one. Rising food prices — and possibly in much of the world rising food scarcity — the moment is now. Wheeler's book will calm you simultaneously cheaper, healthi

— Bill ..., author *Deep Economy*

This is a terrific book, warmly written, funny and smart. Not only do I want to read her gardening book but I immediately found myself fantasizing about hanging out with the author and trading recipes and gardening tricks, that doesn't happen so terribly often — I'm impressed. I really recommend the book, and I'll put it in the food storage section of my store once it is out.

— Sharon Astyk, author of
Depletion and Abundance: Life on the New Home Front
and blogger, www.sharonastyk.com

Robin Wheeler has compiled a terrific resource manual for both rural and urban people concerned with food security and emergency preparedness. *Food Security For the Faint of Heart* is a well researched, informative, and humorous book that will teach and entertain at the same time. It is filled with easy to follow instructions, checklists and stories. I know I will be referencing this book often.

— Bill Elsner, Emergency Planner

FOOD SECURITY for the FAINT of HEART

Keeping
your
Larder full
in Lean times

Robin Wheeler

NEW SOCIETY PUBLISHERS

CATALOGING IN PUBLICATION DATA:
A catalog record for this publication is available from
the National Library of Canada.

Copyright © 2008 by Robin Wheeler.
All rights reserved.

Cover design by Diane McIntosh.
Illustrations: Bernie Lyon.

Printed in Canada. First printing July 2008.

New Society Publishers acknowledges
the support of the Government of Canada through the
Book Publishing Industry Development Program (BPIDP)
for our publishing activities.

Paperback ISBN: 978-0-86571-624-7

Inquiries regarding requests to reprint all or part of
Food Security for the Faint of Heart should be addressed
to New Society Publishers at the address below.

To order directly from the publishers, please call
toll-free (North America) 1-800-567-6772,
or order online at www.newsociety.com

Any other inquiries can be directed by mail to:

New Society Publishers
P.O. Box 189, Gabriola Island, BC V0R 1X0, Canada
(250) 247-9737

New Society Publishers' mission is to publish books that contribute
in fundamental ways to building an ecologically sustainable and just
society, and to do so with the least possible impact on the environment,
in a manner that models this vision. We are committed to doing this
not just through education, but through action. This book is one step
toward ending global deforestation and climate change. It is printed on
Forest Stewardship Council-certified acid-free paper that is 100% post-
consumer recycled (100% old growth forest-free), processed chlorine
free, and printed with vegetable-based, low-VOC inks, with covers
produced using FSC-certified stock. Additionally, New Society purchases
carbon offsets based on an annual audit, operating with a carbon-
neutral footprint. For further information, or to browse our full list of
books and purchase securely, visit our website at: www.newsociety.com

NEW SOCIETY PUBLISHERS
www.newsociety.com

Contents

Acknowledgments

Some people think that writing a book means sitting alone in a room for hours at a time, which is absolutely true, but there are always people running around the periphery making things happen, or there wouldn't be a single book that got out the door.

I offer my great thanks to:

Dania Matiation and Ele Molnar for thinking, "Hmmm, shouldn't you write a book about Food Security?" And to Dania for years of unfailing support.

The Vancouver Coastal Health Authority for agreeing with that idea, and funding the initial project.

Suzy and Frank for starting me off with *Gardening for the Faint of Heart.*

Rochelle Eisen, Organic Goddess, who answers emails in the middle of the night and finds odd bits of info that are brilliant and perfect.

Bill Elsen, the Earthquake Guy, for living in the bush for 12 years so that he could tell us later how to live simply and healthily.

D'Arcy Davis-Case for her experiences in life and warm energy.

Andrea Potter for the cool brining techniques.

Val Luger for making cordials and preserves and medicines and cheese and dried apples from her garden, so that I could learn how graceful and right it all was.

Keira McPhee and Jenn Alexander for cooking me up dozens of cans of delicious soup so I could sit at my keyboard all winter and write.

RoseMarie Pierce, B.Sc.Pharm — How many of us have a Holistic Pharmacist at our fingertips when we really need one to check our herb chapter? I'm a lucky gal.

Bruce and Doneal for resource padding and well-timed espresso shots.

David Richardson at the Butchers Block, for supporting sustainable farms and for donating to my brining skills.

Ananda Howitt for seafood ideas and great cooking.

Justin (Bro) Gilbert for holding my book files safely in case my computer blew up, and for making great garlic mash.

Janet Whitfield for eternal faith.

Carmen and Amy at *Momentum* magazine, for giving me a place to sharpen my teeth.

Al Hudson for bugging me to write at all the right times, even though sometimes I had to remind him it was time to bug me again, and for ancient cucurbita riddles and free booze.

Terry Sunderland for being a really quotable guy.

Bernie Lyon, for once again creating sweet illustrations to perk this book up.

Ingrid Witvoet, Managing Editor at New Society Publishers – gentle handler of writers and their wibblies, for spoiling me.

Lissa Cowan, copyeditor, for nursing things into shape at the very end.

To Mom, Dad, sisters and other family for unconditional love, care packages and understanding.

And to my many friends for bringing a constant stream of gleaned foods: a bag of nuts, a berry pie, a skinned rabbit, fish and mushrooms, apples and cherries, proving over and over the place of love and abundance in our strange world. ·

Introduction

When I was young, my paternal grandparents had a market farm in Surrey, British Columbia. They had an orchard, chickens, and rows of carrots and beans. They had berries and rhubarb, potatoes and corn. At dinnertime, Grandma Wheeler would fire up the woodstove and disappear into her dark, cool pantry. There, she would open jars, cut up a rabbit, send us out for berries or to check for more eggs. Grandpa had soil ground into his hands that would never wash out no matter how he tried. He would sit at the table with one of those hands on each armrest of his big oak chair. His faint handprints are still on that chair, now part of its history, that my older sister refused to have sanded off when she had the rest of the set refinished.

My grandparents were fair, kind, gentle people. Only in retrospect do I realize they did not have a lot of money. To me, theirs was a place of riches — boxes of potatoes and apples, baskets of juicy berries, a pantry full of eggs. I took all of it completely for granted, until they moved onto an urban lot, and there stopped being a place in my existence where food grew on trees.

My second awareness of "food as riches" was in Malaysia in 1968. My family lived at the edge of a village where bananas, papayas, and mangoes dangled from the trees in the yards — even "poor" people had what seemed to be exotic fruit, free for the picking. Fish were brought in with nets from the sea, chickens scratched in gardens and again, while there were not a lot of commercial goods floating around, no one seemed to be starving. Then, after a year-and-a-half, we returned to North America, where our yards were sown with grass and shrubs, and where you had to drive to a store to get food.

Life has, for me (and millions of others), gotten more and more distant from "the garden" ever since. My own move to the country years ago did not protect me from the insanity. It is now illegal for me to buy an organic chicken from the farmer next door, but legal to buy food with over thirty measurable pesticides in it from across the planet. It is a world where the food in my nearest grocery store arrives from all corners of the globe, yet there is no protocol in place for our local farmers to sell their potatoes there. I live in a place where farmers markets and potlucks are being monitored by our "health" departments while dangerous international ingredients are finding their way onto our grocery shelves and where the massive industrial meat recalls are climbing each year. It is a planet of shifting powers and insane regulations, and many of us are feeling a certain lack of control over much that affects us.

This book is about bringing something back home — greater power over our food supply, confidence that what we nourish our children with was grown with care and love, and renewed awareness of our place in the grand scheme of things. I hope this book will remind readers that "power" is not a dirty word. We are powerful beings and can do good things and make change. My grandparents knew that. Their grandparents knew that. Let us not forget it.

— Robin Wheeler, 2008

10 REASONS TO BE FOOD SECURE

1 **Stuff happens.** Earthquakes, trucker strikes, who knows; in an instant, our world could change. We should be better prepared.

2 **It can be difficult for low-income families to afford high quality food.** Fortunately, it costs little to grow nutritious food so having a safe food source nearby (like your own back yard) is a great equalizer.

3 **The World Economy.** What's that all about? Beats them, too! But it's a big, tippy bag of wrestling cats and we hope it doesn't fall over.

4 **Fossil Fuels.** Getting darned expensive, eh? That would explain the high cost of lettuce in January, and of imported olives.

5 **Genetically Modified Organism (GMO) and pesticide use.** Although some say the jury is still out, my vote is in and that is for wholesome food grown without mucking about with anything made in a lab — something we can reproduce in our own back yards, for instance.

6 **Your money stays local.** If your community is strong, you are better off and much safer. Support your local farmers so that they can keep you fed and healthy.

7 **You get enmeshed in your community.** Meet local gardeners and farmers, visit the local organic co-op, go to a canning or earthquake preparedness workshop. Enlarge your circle of connected people.

8 **You do not have to be a drain in times of stress.** In an emergency, the elderly and injured will need all the help they can get. If you can look after yourself, you will not needlessly drain a system that may not have much left to give.

9 **Personal resilience.** Well-prepared people have an edge when handling and recovering from emergencies and trauma. That can't hurt.

10 **Being a new community asset.** In times of stress, we will need many well-informed, experienced people to spread throughout the community. You may be one of them!

CHAPTER 1

The Real Thing — EARTHQUAKE!

*It does not do you good to leave a dragon out of
your calculations if you live near him.*
–J. R. R. TOLKIEN

Some readers might wonder what a chapter on preparing for earth-quakes is doing in a book about food security. The short answer is being food secure is very much like preparing for a natural disaster such as an earthquake. I chose to write about an earthquake because I just happen to live on the quaky coast of British Columbia; however, you can insert hurricane, snowstorm, windstorm, tornado, tsunami or any other natural disaster of your choosing depending on where you live. If you approach food security just as you would prepare for a natural disaster, then you won't feel totally blindsided by the slightly smaller stuff like power outages or losing your job with a house full of hungry kids.

I asked Bill, our local Emergency Program Coordinator, what a typical 6.2 earthquake would look like so that we could really get our hair standing on end, and he said a quake of that caliber lasting "a mere 15 seconds" might cause these problems:

* Roads would become impassable due to fallen hydro lines, bridge collapses, slides, tsunamis or boulders dislodged from retaining walls.

- Hydro and telephone would be offline due to tower and pole collapses.
- Cell phone towers would be jammed and inoperable.
- Water mains would break and rupture. Landslides may obstruct waterways.
- Sewage lines and lift stations would break.
- Natural gas lines would rupture. Fires fed by broken lines would erupt.
- Unattended candles could fall in after shocks causing structure fires. Damaged chimneys would lead to fires and carbon monoxide poisoning.
- People could be trapped in buildings and elevators.
- No bank machines (ATM machines) would be operating.
- Fuel would be reserved for emergency vehicles and generators only.
- Only the most seriously injured would be accepted at hospitals.
- Food deliveries would be curtailed due to infrastructure failures at the ferry terminals, docks etc.
- Initial hoarding of food will cause supplies to rapidly dwindle.
- Restrictions or rationing of food may be implemented.
- Response times from police, fire and ambulance will be significantly reduced or not available.

Darn. I hate it when that happens. But none of this is a big surprise. Folks along the West Coast of North America keep getting warned, over and over, that we are in a prime spot for learning to survive an earthquake. And do we listen? No way! We're from Lotus Land and nothing bad ever happens to us. OK, the power goes out for a bit, and we drive to the nearest restaurant. No problem. And we think to ourselves, an earthquake will not really happen to me because:

1. I'm just a lucky guy/gal.
2. I'm not quite on the epicenter.
3. It will affect everyone else, but not me.
4. I'll be able to handle it with my super human skills.
5. I'm planning my earthquake for about three days after I decide to put a kit together.

Number 4, right after number 1, is my personal favorite. In my imagination, I am using my four-and-a-half-pound Swedish competition ax to chop out the side wall of my kitchen, so that I can reach in for the cans of salmon and soup, and bags of beans and rice, that have conveniently rolled there when the house fell off its foundations. Of course a cooking pot is right there as well, and a wooden spoon (I hate to use metal in my nice pots). And a can opener. And some water. And a cold beer. OK. Never mind.

The Real Thing

We've just had an earthquake showing a 6.2 reading on the Richter scale. Some windows are broken and there's glass on the living room floor. Slip on a pair of heavy shoes to protect your feet. First questions to ask: *Is everyone physically safe? Is the house safe to stay in?* To avoid injury throw folded blankets or couch cushions over broken glass until it can be handled. Check to make sure the gas is turned off and that the circuit breaker to the hot water tank is turned off. Can you see? Where is your flashlight? Oil lamps and lanterns? Don't light any of these until you have turned the gas off and aired the house out. What does the local radio station have to say? Turn on your transistor radio. Check on elders nearby. Look for pets that might be lost. The hydro and phone are out. It's winter and the house is getting cold, very fast.

Time to Take Stock

Oh wait, we were supposed to take stock three months ago, *before* the earthquake. We were supposed to know what we would do in a prolonged emergency. Fortunately, most of us on the West Coast of Canada had a stormy November 2006, and many of us had at least one power outage to practice on. Many of us had to scramble for light and the ability to cook. But now we want to confirm we can find:

- Our gallon of lamp oil, our propane cooker, and our stash of lamps and matches.
- What is in our cupboards, and how the heck to cook it.
- What is in our fridge, and what will spoil the soonest without electricity.
- What is in our freezer, and which of it will need to be eaten first, before it spoils.

Don't open the freezer because your fridge freezer will keep food-stuffs frozen for a couple of days if you don't open it, and your chest freezer will keep even longer. Don't open it until the third day when you're sure the electricity is not coming on soon, and when you are completely ready to deal with the contents.

One of the byproducts of being without restaurants and shopping malls during something as big an earthquake is we learn to make our home-based food supplies last as long as possible. This means keeping waste to a minimum and thinking things through. And it means telling that six-year old that you are not digging the mini pizzas out of the bottom of the freezer for supper. You are instead having the leftover lasagna, because it has meat in it and will spoil first. You will not worry about the cheese for now, or the eggs, which will keep for weeks. You will eat the vegetables in the order you see them wilt, the meat products, and after a couple of days, you will be wary of the mayonnaise and salad dressings, as they do not do well without refrigeration. You will get out a big garbage bag and begin plucking out food before it gets you. Hospitals will be overburdened in an emergency and you will not want to get food poisoning right now.

How to Flush the Toilet When There is no Running Water

You can continue using a flush toilet without running water as long as you have access to a large bucket and a source of outdoor water. And of course you have that because all the water advisory people have been nagging you for two years to have collection barrels under some of your eaves...right?

So you lift the lid off the toilet tank at the back of your toilet, you note where the water level is, then you flush the toilet. When the bowl itself is empty, gently pour your bucket of water into the back until it reaches the previous level. All sound and movement should stop when you hit this level. Replace lid on toilet and place bucket on porch for next movement.

List of Good Things to Have in an Emergency

- A cooler, in case it is winter and you can store fridge items outside.
- Matches or lighter, to be kept dry.
- Lots of cooking oil. Rotate it with your normal supply.
- Salt and other condiments such as sesame oil, tahini, hot sauce, black bean sauce. Emergency food can be boring and you need a good appetite to locate that lost dog.

- Heavy duty tinfoil, to accelerate stove cooking and facilitate woodstove cooking.
- Powdered or canned milk, which will seem yucky but you may be damn glad you have it someday.
- Lots of different kinds of dried noodles and pasta. They cook quickly and can be augmented with a large variety of different foods.
- Canned soups, meats and fish.
- Peanut butter and honey, untouched. If you need them because you ran out in the kitchen, put them right back on your next shopping list.
- Dried beans of any kind. Must be presoaked for half a day and rinsed. This will save hours of cooking time, though they still take hours. This is best for woodstoves where they can simmer in a pan while you are heating the house. Also, best with big jar of tomato sauce.
- Canned nuts. Dried nuts if rotated.
- Dried sunflower or pumpkin seed (need dating and refreshing in your emergency kit).
- Five minute oats and other fast hot cereals.
- The only reason in the world to buy five-minute rice.
- Canned tomatoes.
- If you are used to having caffeine in your body, pack some ground coffee or tea bags, or hot chocolate.
- Bulgur wheat. It cooks fast and you can make tabouleh-type meals.
- Dried falafel powder.
- Sprout seeds.

Tiny Packets of Big Stuff

Who knew that the stringy bits some of us have patiently been pulling out of our deli sandwiches for years have been used to save lives? Well, the Chinese knew, because they've been using sprouted seeds for thousands of years. And James Cook knew in 1768 when he fed his crew sprouts in the form of ground sprouted barley. When they began using sprouts on sailing ships, sailors stopped dying of scurvy. Some smarty pants figured out what a neat package the sprouted seed was — easy to store and carry, sprouted quickly and easily without soil or sun, and magically, in the act of sprouting, its nutrient level got multiplied many times over. Vitamins almost impossible to find in other foods exist in sprouts, and in the case of Vitamin C, can increase by 600% over the value of the seed, and are higher than oranges in this nutrient. Hey — Vitamin K, Laetrile, enzymes and more, and if you have no bacon-cheese burgers in that Earthquake Kit, sprouts will pretty well replace your need for protein. Heck, if you had to, you could pretty well live on sprouts for some time, and would likely end up healthier than many humans are doing on an average North American diet.

I asked Jim Mumm at Mumm's Sprouting Seeds what would be a good type of seed to tuck away in terms of longevity, and he thought the radish, broccoli, broccoli raab, turnip and mustard would be best, followed by alfalfa and clover seed. Of course, we should be eating this stuff instead of just stashing it away for an emergency, but even so, it should last and sprout well for years.

And She Told Us to Eat Our Sprouts...

Wanted: a vegetable that will grow in any climate, rivals meat in nutritive value, matures in three to five days, may be planted any day of the year, requires neither soil or sunshine, rivals tomatoes in vitamin C, has no waste, can be cooked with as little fuel and as quickly as a pork chop.

— Dr. Clive McCay (Quoted in *Add a Few Sprouts* by Martha H. Oliver)

Order of "Certain Death" for Items in Your Freezer

During recent winter storms, few of us in British Columbia had a chance to find out how long food would stay frozen during a prolonged power outage. The answer seemed to be between four to six hours for a fridge freezer and two or three days for a fully loaded chest or stand up freezer. This is not a long time, even if you use all your self-restraint and do not peek in and poke at the side of beef you just purchased. So if you find yourself looking at a gooey mass of thawing food, what are your options? First, you'll have to select a point of no return, where you decide that the power coming back on will not save your frozen food. When food lacks ice crystals, it is too late for it — it is now thawed and needs to enter the Triage Department...

Triage for Fridge and Freezer!

The walking wounded: First, pull out all the foods that may live a few days in a cooler or outside in cold temperatures such as hard cheese, breads and other flour products, butter, fruit and berries and fruit juice. Hold these in the coolest place you can find in your house but you'll have to eat them very quickly. Use the bread for French toast or dry it for croutons.

Need surgery stat? If you are sure that the meat in your freezer has just thawed, then get out that barbecue and cook it up fast! Might as well have a feast and feed your friends and heck, isn't it time to learn to make beef jerky? There is help for meat that is still partly frozen. It can be "brined" in salt water and this will give you several more days. (See sidebar on page 8.)

Time for a proper burial: If you are unsure how long meats and fish have been thawed, they must be taken out and buried deep as quickly as possible. Don't test them on yourself! Let your nose be your guide with your frozen veggies but again, a decent burial is the best thing if there is any doubt at all in your mind that these have been at room temperature for more than eight hours. Don't forget that in times of stress like a power outage, the hospitals and emergency personnel are already pushed to the max, without handling a bunch of food poisoning cases. When in doubt, imagine a houseful of people having diarrhea in a place without a flush toilet. There. That should keep you honest.

If you're thinking this would be a great time to learn pressure canning, you're right! Too bad it takes such prolonged heat — take a look at Chapter 6 on "Storing the Garden Abundance (Top Ten Techniques)" to see if you should be learning alternative food preservation skills right now!

Your Refrigerator

Most raw fruit and vegetables can be moved to a cool place and eaten as they begin to flop. Note that some will keep quite well in a cool room. Eggs will keep for weeks, but make sure they have no cracks in the shell, and break them into a bowl and give a sniff if you haven't been able to keep them cool. But after even a couple of hours at room temperature, some foods become breeding grounds for bugs. Everything that contains any kind of meat, including cold pizza, seafood, chicken or sandwich slices must be discarded. (Phew! Good time to become a vegan!) All cream cheeses and other soft products with eggs and cheese have to go, too. And, sorry, the mayonnaise? Yup. It's over. If you have a garden, bury everything deep and well. If you have spare water, rinse out containers and trays so they don't start to smell and attract flies. You can save your cheese if you cram it into a jar and pour cooking oil over it until it is covered. You can still use this oil for cooking.

Some Like It Cold (And They'd Better, Because That's All They're Going to Get)

One of the big issues in times of drawn out crises like earthquakes and ice storms is lack of fuel for food preparation. If it's winter, when you want a warm tummy, it's easy to keep food cold but there may not be the extra fuel to cook it, and in summer it is easier to face a cold meal but impossible to keep it fresh! There are a couple of ways to handle this such as finding foods that have no storage issues (like canned foods and fruits) or eating foods that require no cooking. Obviously if things get really rough, we will

Brining

Salt curing was used centuries ago and could come in very handy when we want to control the rate at which we eat any precious meat that is bound to thaw during a power outage. The trick is to catch the meat before it loses its ice crystals (if thawed, cook and eat it right away). Make up a brine solution. Best to buy a bag of un-iodized salt now and store it away if you are a meat eater with a freezer. Buy pickling salt, rock salt or water softening salt. Dissolve enough salt into a big jar of hot water until you can float an egg or potato on it. Find any large watertight containers you can such as plastic totes. Even grandma's punch bowl will do in a pinch. Pack your meat tightly into the container and pour the brine solution over the meat until it is covered. Place a big, clean plate over the top if bits want to float. Put this in the coldest place in your house you can find. Pour the brine off every week, stir the brine and pour it back over the meat. If the brine gets stinky or ropy feeling on your fingers, pour it off, wash the meat and make up some fresh brine. This is a result of the temperature being too high, but this may give you a few more days or weeks to cook up your meat. Be warned the meat will be super salty to the taste. It will need soaking and boiling in fresh water to become palatable again, but still may be worth it.

be scraping cold chili out of the inside of a can, but it would be nice to know how to get some solid nutrients into your diet, especially when you're under stress and your body wants real food. Fortunately, there are options. For proteins we have our canned fish, meat and nuts. You can eat alfalfa seeds sprouted and it is pretty well equal to steak in protein, and peanut butter and eggs, until they run out. And please note that careful vegetarians maintain good health.

And there are lots of great carbohydrates available for much of the year, which gives good motivation to have a root garden. A few usual suspects include potatoes, sunchokes, beets, parsnips, turnips, and carrots. All of these veggies will keep outside all winter without refrigeration and the best part is that all of them can be eaten raw. Though it still feels strange to some of us, eating foods raw is the big rage because it's good for you. Raw food is still "alive," important enzymes and vitamins have not been destroyed by heat, and there are fewer cooking and storage issues. Raw foods are naturally cold, and would make poor comfort food on a snowy day, but the nutrients would all be there, richer than you'd ever eaten, zooming through your body and doing their thing. Learning to eat foods raw is easier on the planet because of the saving in cooking fuels, but many of the accompanying condiments we often use to prepare raw foods do have a great big carbon footprint by arriving at our houses from other countries by jet or tanker. However, with just a few condiments and local herbs around, we can certainly get used to some super foods. Think: grated root vegetables tossed with miso gravy, big salads with nuts and sunflower and sesame seeds. Cabbage, peas and beans all taste super on their own.

So if the idea of chomping into a raw potato makes you wish The Big One on some other generation, consider that raw foods are now served at some of the world's most fabulous restaurants.

Beef Jerky

Slice any beef that is defrosting in your freezer into thin slices. Roll the slices thoroughly in pickling salt and pack them away in a container for five days. If you want to get fancy, add honey, sugar or spices to the brine. Then remove, rinse the salt off, and hang the slices (can also be threaded onto string) over a heat source (e.g., camp fire or woodstove) until they are quite dry. These will keep for months in a dry place, in a paper bag or tin. Break pieces into soup or stew. They'll be salty so do not salt the stew!

That might give you a warm glow as you crouch over the grater in your cold kitchen.

Ways and Means of Getting It Hot

In a long-term crunch (and Bill says that when The Big One hits, it will likely be weeks before life resumes any kind of normalcy) we will need to learn how to cook foods using very little fuel, lest it run out before the world starts up again, and without burning our houses down. There are various forms of cooking appliance to choose from, and we can use more than one.

1. **The campfire:** This appliance is about a million years old, and still has its advantages. You can build one anywhere outdoors, out of found items such as rocks and old stove racks. You can use anything for fuel, such as fence posts, old hydro bills and heck, some people even use firewood. With a frying pan, a covered pot and a kettle, you can get a lot of cooking

---

Making Your Own Mayonnaise up in Small Bits as You Need It

When I was without electricity one winter, and the raccoons tore my cooler apart, I had to stop using my precious jar of mayonnaise in case it had gone bad. I kept it around just to look at, to remind me of a better world, and occasionally used the jar (cooled outside on a cold night) to take the bruising out of an injury, but finally knew it was over when my friends drove up and caught me nestling my mayo jar in my arms, out by the back woodshed. I had to show them my bleeding thumb to prove the relationship was real, but I knew I had gone too far. They recognized that jar from last time. Me and my mayonnaise had been found out. That night, I quietly said goodbye to my mayo jar. That's about the day I knew I had been in the bush too long.

Ingredients
One or two egg yolks (warmed to room temperature)
½ to 1 tablespoon of vinegar or lemon juice
Pinch of salt, pepper and/or Dijon mustard
Whisk it really well.

Very slowly, drop by drop at first, drizzle in 1 cup olive or veggie oil, whisking like crazy and taking your time. Taste it and check the texture when most of the oil is in, and then add more lemon, salt or oil depending on your tastes. If you have no cold place to store this, eat all your messiest mayo foods right away, invite the raccoons over for their favorite spread, and then toss any leftovers.

---

done. Those are the assets. The downside is that there is much smoke produced, you might have to sit in the rain to tend it, there is huge risk of spreading fire if you don't situate your campfire carefully, and there is a constant need to feed the darn thing with dry fuel. It's also difficult to light in the rain or snow. Otherwise, it has kept humans warm and fed for donkey's years.

2. **Woodstove:** I love my woodstove. It dries and warms my boots on wet wintry days, dehydrates the trays of food hanging overhead, keeps the house toasty and when the power is out, I can heat up soup and have a hot drink. Not all of us have a woodstove but if you are building or renovating a home and have the opportunity to include one, this is an excellent backup and replacement for several appliances. The drawback is the huge expense of installation, and, of course, a decent woodpile must await you outside. It's a pollution hog when you just want a cup of coffee in the morning, but offers several techniques for cooking meals. For instance, you can wrap veggies up in tinfoil and poke them into a corner of the ashes to cook, you can lay food on a rack and introduce it when the flames have gotten low and you have a good bed of coals. You can use the cooking surface for any pot or kettle, and the long slow heat of it is excellent for cooking soups from scratch or thawing out frozen lasagna.

3. **Propane camp stove:** People who camp for recreation are way ahead of us if they've had any experience cooking in the outdoors on a portable propane stove. They know how to assemble the parts and safely get the gas running. They are confident about using it in wind and rain. If we have no other opportunity for heating food available to us, we should buy a small camp stove, extra fuel, and we should have a little dinner party out on the back balcony once a month so that we're confident with the components and how to use the stove. Remember when cooking with finite things like fuel canisters to have everything chopped up and ready before you begin, to cut things up small, and to cook only one serving at a time if there is no way to refrigerate leftovers.

4. **The barbecue or hibachi:** Some of us actually do have a ready cooking appliance sitting right outside. If you do own a

barbecue, be like my baby sister and check that you have lots of fuel at all times, because your husband might not do it (It's his fault.) And remember that barbecuing always has to occur outside, and that you cannot turn coals "off" and "on," so plan well by using remaining heat to boil eggs for later or heat water for a nightly wash and a cup of tea.

Eating Quick-Cook Foods

It was late December 1996, and I was living in my little building in a small clearing way up Mount Elphinstone. That was the winter of the freak, waist-deep snowfall, the one that took out the water, the electricity, and my woodshed, all in a one-hour period. Thank goodness I had poured my morning coffee just before that little chain of events! And best of all, after hand digging my firewood out all morning, I had an opportunity to try out Mom's Christmas Care package, full of instant coffee, canned chili, soup and stew. Just toss a can of something over the heat and instant dinner! There would be no harm in this if I didn't get crazy thirsty after each meal and have to melt some snow. And if I'd known I would be relying on the stuff, I would have balanced my food groups better, and gone for a little variety. But one-pot cooking did keep the dishes down, which was a good thing because once the waterline froze, the dishes started to smell and it was hard to flush the toilet without finding a whole big bucket of thawed snow to pour down the back of it...and this is just a little nagging moment, because guess who keeps barrels and tanks of water all over the property now?

Even if we do have a full tank of propane or a bag of briquettes, we will have no idea how long we'll be before the next shopping trip for more. Better to get all the mileage we can out of what we have.

Some tips:

* Cut food in small pieces so it will cook faster. Vegetables like carrots and potatoes, and all types of meats prove this out. For instance, grated foods like potato pancakes cook faster than any other kind of potato.
* Keeping the lid on a pot keeps heat in and reduces cooking time.
* Turn heat down under pots as soon as desired heat is reached.

- Wrapping veggies in tinfoil for roasting, shiny side in, also speeds things up, as does poking a large nail into them.
- Use the heaviest pots you have, give food a good blast of heat and then turn the heat off and let the food cook within the walls of the pot.

Other tips

- Bulgur wheat: Just add boiling water to cover, put a lid on, and wait thirty minutes.
- Rice: Bring to a boil, turn heat off and put in an insulated box and do not remove lid for at least half an hour.
- Pasta: Soak in water until soft. Make a cold salad or just heat with condiments.
- Quick Oats: This is a good reason to have some maple syrup or brown sugar or raisins tucked away. Oats and other grains make a quick warm meal that can be cooked within minutes on a hot stove but will cook, in time, on a tepid wood stove as well.

Steam-Fry (Instant) Noodles

These now come in little square packs, but also come in bigger bags for much less money. You have to make your own "spice packet" for the big bags and soy or tahini with some sesame oil seems to do it. These noodles store forever and are fast to cook. The trick is to put in lots of veggies to raise them to some sort of acceptable nutrient level. Otherwise, they're just comfort food! No harm in a little comfort, but putting your water on first, and slicing carrots, broccoli, green onions and mushrooms into the pot before adding your noodles and spice packet will easily up your daily levels of real food.

Egg Swirl Soup

Ingredients
Any amount or type of steam fried Asian noodles
Any amount of carrots, mushrooms, green
    onions, broccoli, kale stems, cabbage
Spice packet, or sesame oil with tahini or soy sauce
1 egg

Pour a couple of cups of water into a pot. Slice in vegetables like carrots, green onions, broccoli, mushrooms, kale stems and cabbage. Bring this to a boil and then break the noodles into bits and drop them in. Stir this in, add the spice packet or soy and sesame oil, and when the noodles are soft, which should be only minutes, break an egg over the pot and stir it into the glop. Stir it well in, let it cook for a couple of minutes, turn the heat off, and eat! This should take less than ten minutes of cooking time. Any variations on this are good. Sometimes I boil the noodles soft and pour off the water and throw them in a bowl. Then I put a half cup of water back in the pot and chop celery thin into it, plus the spice packet. I cook that till the liquid is almost gone, pour the noodles back over it, drop some sesame oil and chopped onion greens and if I have a tiny bit of organic chicken or fish around, that can go in as well. Takes a bit longer to cook and has that almost impossible to find local celery, but is really yummy.

Wilted Greens

Strangely good, it satisfies the need for grease and salt. Chop kale, wild greens, sliced onions, chard and cabbage (or just one or two of the above) into a frying pan. Add a tablespoon of olive oil, one tablespoon of sesame oil, a couple of tablespoons of water and a splash of soya sauce. Cook on medium for just a few minutes with the lid on, and eat. This would probably work with any veggies.

Kath's Tomato Cheese Soup
(Cans from Your Emergency Kit and Moldy Cheese)

This is the only soup that comes out of a can that you'll find in this book, and the reason I hold it in such esteem is that a dear friend made a big pot of this and put it in my fridge minutes before I quit smoking. Then she left town, which was wise. The thing is, the soup was rib-sticking comfort food, and came from things you might find at the back of the cupboard and fridge. She knew it would be easy for me to reproduce it in a hurry if I felt a craving coming on. I tried smoking the dried soup, but it just made me dizzy.

Ingredients

1 tin stewed tomatoes (or equivalent in home
  cooked tomatoes)

1 tin corn

1 tin condensed tomato soup, diluted with one
  tin of milk

3 big green onions, chopped fine

¼ teaspoon chili powder

A giant handful of grated cheddar cheese, or
  more.

Mix all but the cheese and green onions together in your big
soup pot. Heat it on medium for about an hour with the lid
on. Add the cheese and onions and stir well. Serve with more
grated cheese on top. This is a good recipe for a wood stove.

Pasta Noodles

Well, what can we say? Pasta noodles can get reasonably cooked
over even a tepid fire, and with a jar of sauce poured over it, is a
meal that can be ready in minutes. This is an excellent reason to
tuck some canned tomato products into your emergency storage
space. The parmesan cheese will have to be hidden in the back of
the freezer and pulled out last, sodden but still alive and usable,
for these little treats.

Stove-Top Baking

If you do have a woodstove or dependable fire, try baking inside
of a roasting pan. Put a couple of inches of gravel in a big roasting
pan, place a layer of foil on top of that, place your cake or bread
pan on top of this. Put the lid on the roasting pan and test in one
hour.

Bannock

Ingredients

4 cups flour

4 teaspoon baking powder

1 teaspoon salt

4 tablespoons oil

Mix ingredients and add water until you have a doughy
consistency, and then knead for 10 minutes. Brown sugar,

cinnamon or dried fruit can be added. Oil your heavy frying pan, form the dough into small cakes and dust with flour. Place the bannock into the pan and shift them every few minutes to prevent burning. When the base is cooked solid enough, flip the bannock once. Each bannock takes about 10 minutes to cook.

Essay: A Few of My Favorite (Survivalist) Things

Sometimes, such as on the (verge/apex/end) of a threatened (war/invasion/friendly takeover), my city friends try to get a rise out of me by telling me that if there is ever a cataclysmic event that threatens our food supply, dozens of city folk will promptly swim across the inlet and stampede through my garden, demanding to be fed. Of course I have a pat answer for this: There isn't enough for all of us, so we're all going down, and besides, they wouldn't know where the food was if they were standing on it.

If I was dishing out advice to those crazy city folk at a time like that, it would be to always plan for an emergency food supply several months *before* an unpredicted disaster. It would be much better if many people knew how to garden for themselves, and how to choose nutritious crops that last (or can be stored) over a long period. Then they wouldn't end up here, trampling my potatoes.

Next, I would have to take my own advice. First off, if I was considering living through some type of food shortage, I would start with the realization that I could not grow all my foodstuffs, likely just enough to supplement other supplies. So my first move would be to purchase a big jug of olive oil and tuck it away in the back of a cupboard. I would check my dry goods, and buy a large sack of organic rice, not the stuff that takes forty-five minutes to cook. And I might get some quick oats and other grains that take little cooking. Then I would plant lots of beans in my garden — all types of beans...black beans, scarlet runners, soy and soup beans. I would tuck them between bushes and stick them behind the flowers. I would train them up the carport wall and along the railings. And in the fall, I would take these out of the dry pods and store them in jars. I would do the same with peas, because they are also a healthy food and last a long time in their dried state. I would plant lots of high nutrient greens. The stuff with reds and purple in the leaves are higher in nutrients than the plain green. I would make sure there was kale and chard, purple broccoli and mustards. Greens, per week of growing time, would be the quickest nutrient boost off the block in an emergency. But we don't know when disaster might strike, so I would plant lots of things that would live under the soil all winter so that I could dig them as I needed them, such as carrots and beets and parsnips. And lots of potatoes. I would grow things like garlic and onions and squash that could be cured in the fall sunlight and then stored for literally months in my home.

I would certainly make a visit to the library and borrow some books on native plants, so I would find out which roots were good to eat. And don't laugh at that — I have a funny feeling there would be fewer hemorrhoids and bowel diseases if more people ate things right out of the ground.

> **Hey Kids!**
>
> Next time your parents tell you you're disorganized, that you never plan, and that you'll grow up to be a telephone sanitizer if you don't get it together, first remind them that hey, your prefrontal lobes aren't fully developed yet so you're incapable of thorough planning, and then, ask them how the Earthquake Kit is coming along!! Ask them, if there is an earthquake, if you will have to eat wall plaster and sawdust. You'll have them down flat. They'll have to go off somewhere and think of a snappy comeback. But tell them not to bother. You'd rather they spent the time packing an Earthquake Kit.

I would spend more time reading about edible parts of garden plants, too, such as how to cook the shoots of my day lilies, and how to make tea out of rose hips — a rare source of winter Vitamin C.

I know I would not like to live like this, but that I would feel less helpless if I had some tricks up my sleeve. But we all know that food is not going to be the only thing we miss in an emergency. It's the lack of caffeine, and Prozac, and alcohol and cigarettes — the unseen monkeys we share our lives with — that is what is going to make the glass break on those city streets.

My potato patch is probably quite safe. So get out there, you survivalists, and start figuring out where the Good Food is going to come from — while there is still time to practice.

Goals

- Put a blank piece of paper on your fridge and begin adding foods that you can put away for an emergency.
- Figure out approximately how much food is consumed a day in your home and plan to have at least a two-week supply of grub put away.
- Begin buying cooking oil one full bottle ahead (buying the next bottle as soon as you open this one) so that you always have back up.
- Begin adding more food items to the list that you buy new as soon as you open the last jar. It's a good habit and will see you through short-term problems.
- Create one back-up cooking system for your home such as a propane stove, fire pit or hibachi. Have friends over, and practice cooking on your new system.
- Ask some practiced campers to show you their techniques and try them out at home.

Resources

Braunstein, Mark Mathew. *Sprout Garden: Grower's Guide to Gourmet Sprouts*. Toronto: Book Publishing Company, 1999.
    The author presents convincing information about how to grow legumes and seeds and the science behind it.

Robertson, Jon and Robin Robertson. *Apocalypse Chow: How to Eat Well When the Power Goes Out*. New York: Simon & Schuster, Inc. (Simon Spotlight Entertainment), 2005.
    Fun for those stocking up purely from the supermarket, who have a decent income, and who like their emergencies with a dash of canned chilies and some red wine.

Talmage Stevens, James. *Making the Best of Basics: Family Preparedness Handbook*. Salt Lake City: Gold Leaf Press, 1997.
    This is a great resource for those worried about long-term emergency preparedness, covering many resource needs besides food.

CHAPTER 2

Stockpiling

If my Grandma Wheeler was alive, I would phone her up and ask her what the word was back then for making sure your house had lots of food put away. I don't think she would have said, "Oh, that was just a little stockpiling, dear." Today, that wise gesture of packing several weeks' worth of supplies up has connotations of paranoia, and perhaps a stink of selfishness. How did such a great concept become such a dirty word? Most of us will have to learn how to get through a truckers' strike, an ice storm or a long-term layoff, and having a stash put away does no harm.

For Grandma, it meant sitting safely in her house and having healthy grub at her fingertips. It meant not wasting a squash or a bean or a berry all summer, but then, not wanting for one later on. Of course, she had space for that, as most folks did in the past. Even without freezers, there were generally basements, pantries, sheds and root cellars. Today, our homes are built without that wondrous space where you just fling a door open and rows of cans and jars shine out at you. It actually seems a bit quaint to wish for a room like this, and even here on the fringes of town where I live, I am constantly explaining to people why I have food put away. Why do I have five pounds of garlic in my cupboard? Because that's how much I grew and that's where it lives. And I have lots of tinned tomatoes because it's cheaper by the flat, and I have lots of tinned fish and fruit in case I get snowed in again and get tired of soup and beans. This seems elementary in the boonies, but raises eyebrows in the city. But there are other agendas at work here. I don't spend much time shopping any-more, and I'm happy about that. I don't burn up fossil fuels shoot-ing up and down the hill for a few items. It just feels good, and I know Grandma Wheeler would agree.

Men Will Come with Guns and Take Your Food

I think stockpiling becomes a dirty word when it causes suffering for others. I once heard of a man who ran into a corner store and bought all the candles there, because he wanted to sell them off at a profit when the coming windstorm caused a power failure. As that example shows, people can stockpile resources to keep them from others, for their own gain. This makes them feel secure, but I wouldn't want to be in the shoes of the person holding all the goodies when crisis strikes.

Stockpiling is a dandy cure for Seasonal Affective Disorder (SAD), too! Here's why...

Controlled Fall

I read somewhere (and "somewhere" is a pretty dusty furrow in my mind) that the reason we get a tug at our hearts when we hear the geese heading out for the winter, is that the call pulls on an ancient part of our brains, from a time we understood and paid heed to the messages of fellow beings, that it was time to begin preparations for the cold. The cells in our bodies know what needs doing when the geese leave, that we need to find a warm place to prepare for the new season, to either follow our clever goose friends, or hoard some food and nestle in for the long haul. Only then will our souls quiet down.

I began responding to that call a few years ago, and I now slide into winter with a much calmer heart. Instead of ruing the short days and rainy evenings, I fill up the woodshed, pack some potatoes into the crawl space, shell the last of the beans into their jars, and by the time the frost begins to nibble, I'm quite content to lie on the couch and scratch my belly for a couple of months. And a couple of summers ago, when most of my house was pretty much built and a lot of my tiny farm had some food squirting out of it, I actually did the "D" word ("Domestic" for those of you who don't use the word that often) and bought myself some canning jars.

That first summer of testing out my hidden domestic, I headed down to Val's old farm and she taught me to pressure can a salmon or two. I brought the jars home and lined them up in my cupboard. I admired them and they gleamed back at me. Then I tripped over the horseradish plant in the new herb bed, and pulled up a couple ⟋

And this is where this particular topic becomes a red hot button in my house. Several community members have reminded me that if I put up food for the winter, "Men will come with guns and take your food." Well! The first time I heard that, you can imagine the huff that caused in me. Who were these poorly raised sods, that they sit on their bums, watching bad sitcoms no doubt, only to come and loot my last three jars of peach chutney when times got tough? Who raised these people? I wanted a word with their mothers and fathers. And when the fourth person said this to me, right after apple butter time, well, I got into a real snit. I decided to go find these people lurking away outside of our healthy community, and give them a piece of my mind.

They could be saving their own food, or better yet, helping others save food and taking home some of the spoils. They could

of roots and made some little jars of sauce. This is a problem because I haven't seen a roast beast for some time, but heck, I can trade them up. And they looked exciting lined up in the fridge.

A few days later, the wood truck hit my little apple tree and knocked a decent haul to the ground, so I made a batch of apple butter, and with the juice, made some jelly. I lined those jars up, too. I cannot tell you how satisfying it is to gaze on a row of full preserve jars. Then the peach tree starting looking a little sloppy, what with all those peaches hanging off the side, and so I pulled out my recipe books and dragged another box of jars up from the crawlspace. It was at this point that a friend said to me, "Hah — Why don't you just put all that stuff in the freezer? You think the world's going to end or something?" O.K., it wasn't those exact words, but it made me wonder what bygone era I was trying to slide back into.

And then that very week I reached into my refrigerator freezer and ran smack into a pile of soggy, deflated, lukewarm bags. I gave a big sigh to the mass of thawed berries and beans, the limp salmon and sad tofu dogs. I went out into the garden and dug some holes and gave all my carefully gleaned freezer food a proper burial. It took a long time because the soil is so dry and rocky and it was still pretty warm outside. Then I pulled out my recipe book and went and sat under my peach tree. I felt a bit like an early scientist discovering exactly why you are supposed to shut the barn door before the horses run out of it. I made an even longer list of foods I can prepare that will sit there for years as good as new. And I leaned back against the tree and dreamt of future, winter evenings, the taste of warm peaches in honey syrup, with the sound of muffled rain beating the roof in the background. And it was good.

be using their great skills to make their community strong, and be part of it, and then I would have less to worry about. Instead of being my problem, they could be someone else's solution. Yes, on a tiny scale, and even a large one, this could work. I earmarked a couple of the more likely culprits and planned my next visit. My clever friend Terry heard my rant and thought me up a slogan for my upcoming campaign. "Women Will Come with Food and Take Your Guns." I liked it and I liked the planetary shift I felt when I said it. It sounded like a big job, but I was willing to chip away at it for a few years. And if anyone would like to help with this project, that would be great.

Women Will Come with Food and Take Your Guns

I just had another dreadful meeting with Bill Elsner, our local earthquake guy. (He doesn't cause them, he just helps us figure out how to live through them.) Bill is a stockpiling pro, because he spent years in the northern bush, saving every bit of food for winter and hating waste and knowing the value of a bit of dried orange peel in a teapot or some real fruit in the middle of a snow-in. What makes these meetings so dreadful is staying on my tedious, time-constrained track while Bill tells great tales of raising little children in the frozen north, living on fish and tenacity and preserved garden food. It was very hard work, but he looks pretty fit and healthy for it. And I love the stories. My other source for this chapter, equally dreadful to stay on track with, is my friend D'Arcy, who also used to live way in the boonies and shopped once a year (read that again, folks — once a year) and had to think of everything she needed because it was a long boat trip out for a can of artichoke hearts. And yup, she raised her kids that way, too.

THEY ALL LAUGHED when they heard I was putting food away...

Thoughts for the stockpiler to keep in mind.

1. No need to feel or act as if you are doing something out-of-the-ordinary. Stocking up food is not a freakish act — it's smart. We have thousands of years of history of it. Bees do it. Squirrels do it.

2. Keep a low profile and just do what makes you feel good. You'll feel less stressed knowing you have something tucked away.

3. They'll be sorry, nyah, nyah, told you so, and so on....

The following short (but mighty) list below was given to me by these two bright, lovely people who also have in common the fact they have never watched a single episode of "Survivor."

* Date all your perishables.
* Flour and nuts go rancid. Keep them very cool, use them fast.
* Watch for mice and insect damage.
* Have a method for rotation.

Stockpiling isn't easy for low income earners, because obviously it's damned expensive to buy bags and bags of food to push into cupboards and cram into closets. But if you open your mind to the idea, and make it a consistent habit to pick up two jars when you need one, to buy a case when you have a bit of extra cash, or to buy in bulk if you can possibly afford it, the advantages begin to roll in. You suddenly realize you don't have to run out so often to shop, prices are lower when you buy in quantity, and when the lights go out...you're set.

Stockpiling Tips

* When buying one jar or bag of something, always buy a second whenever you can, and put the spare one away.
* List-making is an excellent habit. Keep some paper taped to your fridge and make notes when you see an item getting low in the cupboard.
* Begin buying bigger bags of rice (one size up from usual), more toilet paper at a time, more tea bags and oil.
* Watch for sales so that you can save money, but only buy what you eat.
* Don't wait to run out of a product. Get in the habit of buying ahead while you still have lots left at home.

Below is a letter from D'Arcy, talking about her top five tips for stockpiling.

Shopping Once a Year

Once upon a time when my children were very young, we lived in Dawson's Landing, Rivers Inlet in British Columbia. This was considered isolation, with the only access being by boat or float plane. Our family was allowed one "grub run" a year. With four people to feed, it took some planning to figure out what we would need to eat for that period. So once a year, I would go shopping at Woodward's. I chose what I knew we already ate, and if I reached for one can or box of something, then I would calculate that I needed a carton. My grocery shipment was sent up on the freight boat.

The five things I learned in these five years about stockpiling food (most of them in the first year) were:

One: Consider the Basics

What does the family like to eat? What are your normal every-day meals? Variations are necessary, but if you miss the basics, it is boring to eat smoked oysters for two weeks. Our general menu looked something like this.

Breakfast: Oatmeal, red river cereal, cream of wheat porridge, milk, juice, toast. **Weekends:** French toast, pancakes/sausage, crepes.

Lunch: Soup and sandwiches.

Dinner: Meat, starch (rice/potatoes/pasta) vegetables, fruit dessert.

Saturday was always something easy like a pizza or chili con carne and corn bread. Sunday was traditionally a carnivorous roast, and a special dessert. But I also had to shop for the yearly Christmas, birthdays, Easter, picnics, and parties which would not in the least resemble Christmas, birthday, Easter, picnics, and parties without that special something to feast on.

Two: Resist Processed Foods

Lets face it. When you don't have to spend time shopping, you have a lot more time to cook. Variety is in the spices, and the raw materials. I did buy a case of chocolate cake mix the first year, and the mice enjoyed eating their way through the boxes. We thought our scratch cakes tasted better anyway, especially the chocolate cardamom cake!

From scratch is less expensive, takes less space, offers the variety of your imagination and skill, doesn't have unpronounceable additives and is way more fun to make — and educational! My son learned to cook "gourmet" in Rivers Inlet. He wanted a chemistry set for Christmas, but I had already bought him a remote controlled plane. I told him that cooking was chemistry, and the kitchen, the lab.

Three: Storage is Crucial

Cool, dry and secure are the mantras of the food sequestarians. I had a basement, which offered the first two, but was home to generations of very intelligent rats. Cute, but they could do a lot of damage in an afternoon. Weevils were a drag. They were in my oatmeal one year, and I just sifted them out when the family was asleep. Promise not to tell them.

Large metal and glass containers were like gold. By the end of my first year, I had all my used gallon pickle and olive jars as well as dozens I picked up from a friend who owned a restaurant. I still remember the day I found the metal lard pails behind a bakery when I was down on a food shop, and took ten of them down to the freight company in a taxi.

My basement food stash was a joy to visit. I was lucky enough to have shelves for the jars and the canned goods. No cardboard though as it attracts the mice, and seems to absorb any dampness that might be present.

I canned salmon, because we inherited an old pedal driven canner from some old-timers who left the Inlet. I had a good pressure cooker and canned lots of fish. Our favorite (and might I say what we are probably remembered for) is the canned salmon with a small piece of smoked salmon in the middle to add taste. Yum! I canned berries in glass jars, sometimes meat if it happened by, and applesauce from the old trees at the derelict hospital.

Potatoes, carrots, onions and apples kept well. I had two old washtubs with lids and kept them in there with sand. The carrots I wrapped in the children's completed school assignments. I learned how to make sour cabbage, and produced incredible cabbage rolls.

Four: Accept Nature's Abundance

The ocean, the garden and the forest offered up an abundance of things that I had to learn to cook, and the family had to learn to eat. The First Nations folks at the head of the Inlet were wonderful in helping me to identify what was edible and how to cook it. Berries were plentiful, and we made pies, jams and jellies for the whole year. Fish was on the menu at least three days a week — wonderful snapper, salmon, crab, clams, abalone and prawns. Occasionally a local would get a deer and the meat would be shared. My garden did better each year, and the Brussels sprouts were lurking under the snow, awaiting our Christmas dinners.

Five: Emergency Recipes

We didn't have power unless we put on the generator, mainly to vacuum or if people were coming to visit. We would go to bed when it was dark, and wake up when it was light. My father visited and made me a battery lamp so I could read at night.

I cooked with propane. But these days, with my electric stove, when the power goes out I revert to what I can cook on the wood-stove. Bannock with fried Spam.

Rations — this is how D'Arcy figured out her needs:

Starch: flour, bran, oats, rice	Seeds: sunflower, sesame		
Sweet: sugar (brown, white, icing), honey, corn syrup,	Nuts	Eggs: dried eggs, egg whites (tins)	
Risers: yeast, baking powder, baking soda, cream of tartar	Fruit: dried apples, apricots, prunes, cranberries, raisins	Milk: powder, canned milk	Grease: tinned butter, tinned Crisco, lard, olive oil, vegetable oil
Spices: salt, pepper, turmeric, dill, celery seed, etc. (Mix your own)	Vegetable	Meat: canned chickens, ham, bacon, dehydrated hamburger, Spam (everything but fish)	cocoa

And here is a brief sample of the quantities that D'Arcy bought these supplies in:
- 140 pounds of flour
- 1 pound of yeast
- 10 pounds coarse salt
- 5 pounds table salt
- 3 cases butter (from Denmark)

Meat:

- 3 cases bacon (from Denmark)
- 1 case horrid meat (Spamesque)
- 1 case canned chickens
- 1 case canned ham
- 2 cases hamburger (dehydrated)

Things to Do

- Begin stockpiling the foods that will be most important to you (such as canned soup) *before* the chocolate cake mix.
- Learn to overlap your food stores. As you take something out, remember to jot on your food list on the fridge to buy some more.
- Learn to rotate the old can from the back of the cupboard to the front when you empty your grocery bags each shopping day.
- Don't forget the toilet paper!

CHAPTER 3

Buying Organic
on a Budget

My Emergency Coordinator Guy, Bill, says it is silly to worry about food being organic if we are facing an immediate crisis, and of course, he is right. We will eat what is convenient, then we will eat what we have to, then we will scrape scum off the inside of the fridge. But if we are thinking of food security in terms of the big picture, then secure food is that which is grown locally and with available inputs (Do you see a phosphate mine in your town? An oil refinery for those trucks? Didn't think so.) That way, the birds and bees are safe and happy, conscientious farmers are getting our dollar, and we are supporting keeping a larger segment of our farmland as clean as is possible. Besides, anyone reading this who has trouble affording food can just take out the word "organic" and will usually end up with the information being useful.

When people make the switch to organic, they usually get a shock over some of the prices. Why is this stuff so expensive, they ask? Are those crazy farmers saving up for their own helicopter pad? But no, organic growers, especially the small scale local growers who we want to support and encourage, are out there in the rain hand-digging weeds so they won't have to spray, hand picking bugs so they won't have to spray, improving the soil for healthy plants, so they won't have to spray. Doing things the proper old-fashioned way takes time and energy, but leaves resilient healthy earth that will be productive for decades to come.

And small local farmers generally have mortgages and plumbing problems, just like you, only without a steady income.

One thing a bag of hard-earned organic food does is make you appreciate it as a valuable commodity. You no longer slather butter on a piece of toast so thickly when you are paying for the farmer's extra work in bringing you a clean product. When you're paying good money for the farmer to do it right, you're bringing home food of value. You tend not to stick it into the back of the fridge and forget about it. You waste less, toss more veggie ends into the stir-fry, take better care of that bag of grains. In fact, the price of organics may make people more respectful of "real" food in several ways. People paying more for good food start to look at waste differently. The stale corn chips are put aside to be dried out in the toaster oven with a layer of cheese, and hard old cheese at the end of a package is scraped off and grated into the potato leek soup. Seeing food as valuable and worthy brings us back to a respectful relationship with the material that builds our body cells and fuels our brains.

Really Cheap Food on Sale Now!!

When my loyal old dog turned twelve years old, I went to the local pet shop to buy her some geriatric dog food. Although she spent most of her time sleeping, and didn't seem to benefit much from my attentions, I felt it would be nice of me to follow all the conventional steps as she entered her decline.

The pet store man stopped me from buying the kibble for retired rovers and talked me into a big bag of very expensive regular dog food instead. He told me it was better for her. He told me it was worth every penny for a healthy dog, and that there would be reduced vet bills. He told me that in four days on this feed, she would be dancing the fandango. I rolled my eyes, but I finally bought a bag of it to shut him up. And I went home feeling like a good mother. I fed her whatever the heck was in that bag. Four days later, at about 6:32 AM, she woke me up out of a dead sleep. She was at my bedside, dancing the fandango. "Wow," I said, "Waiter, I'll have what she's having!" I looked long and hard at this dog. If four days of highly nu-tritious food could do this for her, what would it do for elders in seniors' homes? People who ate at fast food joints? The homeless? Teenagers? But then I remembered: Food quality is not a human priority.

I live in a world where we fight for the cheapest food pos-sible — where people I know actually boast over how little they pay for their children's breakfast cereal. I live in a world where the value that farmers struggle to squeeze out of the tired earth is measured in pennies per pound instead of vitamins per ounce, where meat animals are fed waste products to increase profits, and where people become sicker while surrounded by food. The stuff we run our precious bodies on is valued pretty poorly in our society. Cheap is best — SALE! SALE! SALE. No nu-trients need inquire. Heck, did someone just say "nutrient?" What a concept!

It would be an interesting world if my pet shop fellow turned his head to feeding humans properly. He would measure how many vitamins and minerals we needed and how many carbohydrates we used per day at different stages of our lives. After all, pet food people know that puppies and elders have different needs from each other. He would make sure that lac-tating mothers got extra calories and minerals, and he would know when to squeeze in some nutrient rich fats. Maybe by foregoing that latte, the plastic doodads for the kids and the extra video, we could afford to be nibbling on nutrient-dense foods. Our eyes would brighten and our coats would glow. We would get up at 6:32 AM and dance the fandango. Just think.

So how can we switch to healthier foods, and then be able to af-ford them?

The price we pay for organics more closely reflects the true cost of doing healthy business, but it can also make you recon-sider the foods you will choose to buy. Meats and butter are deadly expensive in organic form, but fortunately, it is good for us to eat way less of them, so treasuring every ounce, or deciding not to eat much or any at all of them does us no harm.

Some people make the switch in small jumps. First, they begin buying organic fruit and greens. Then they start buying milk and cheese. Then cereals. And one day, the funny thing is, it's easier to just JUMP. Your body seems to suddenly know what's good for it.

Several Methods for Eating on a Budget

Just skip the worst of the expensive foods. For instance, North Americans eat way more meat than is necessary, and it can take up a lot of room on a food budget. Although many people cannot imagine giving up meat forever, it can seem more agreeable to find ways to use way less of it. For instance, chopping a bit of cooked chicken over a stir fry can give it a delicious edge with very little meat involved. Small flakes of ham in a pea soup can stretch a slice into several meals. Chopping a hunk of meat into a vegetable stew will give it more mileage. Chop a single piece of bacon into an omelet instead of putting several rashers on the side. Add a bit of salmon to a salad instead of eating a complete steak. Other cultures are way better at this, with no suffering to their health, and it does seem shocking, when coming back from a trip to Asia, to see a whole hunk of meat taking up half a plate.

As far as skipping the worst of the *bad* food goes, the Consumer's Union in the United States has named the ten following foods the non-organic ones to avoid if you are trying to reduce pesticide levels in you or your children.

Winter Squash	Wheat	Strawberries
Green beans	Celery	Apples
Peaches	Grapes	Spinach
Pears		

Here are details taken from the Consumers Union website on just a couple of the above named foods to help us understand the implications of our food choices:

Peaches

Summer's blushing fruit contains high residues of iprodione, classified as a probable human carcinogen by the Environmental Protection Agency (EPA) and methyl parathion, an endocrine disruptor and organophosphate (OP) insecticide. Methyl parathion has caused massive kills of bees and birds. According to Consumer Reports, single servings of peaches "consistently exceeded" EPA's safe daily limit for a 44-pound child.

Winter Squash

Dieldrin, a chlorinated, carcinogenic insecticide, exceeded the safe daily limit for a young child in two-thirds of positive samples. Another potent carcinogen, heptachlor, also showed up.

DDT and its breakdown product, DDE, were detected in baby food squash.

Green Beans

Green Beans can contain acephate, methamidophos and dimethoate (three neurotoxic OPs), and endosulfan, an endocrine-disrupting insecticide, which showed up in baby food, too. Acephate disorients migrating birds, throwing them off course.

Grapes

U.S. grapes contain methyl parathion and methomyl, a carbamate insecticide listed as an endocrine disruptor; imports may contain dimethoate.

Strawberries

The enhanced red color of strawberries comes from the fungicide captan, a probable human carcinogen that can irritate skin and eyes, and is highly toxic to fish. While the lethal soil fumigant methyl bromide doesn't show up on the fruit, it has harmed California farm workers, and depletes the ozone layer.

Some foods are not labeled as "organic" but are naturally just very clean foods and it is good to know what these are. Italian olives are frequently grown in the same manner as they were five-hundred years ago (before pesticides) so they are a good bet for a clean oil. Many old European wineries refuse to become certified organic, but use ancient, scrupulously clean standards. Your local liquor store employees may surprise you by knowing which wines are technically organic and you can compare prices from there. Besides this, new international regulations will make it illegal for organic farms to call their food organic unless they pay to certify, which will make this term too expensive for small or marginal farms to afford its use, even though they may be growing clean-as-possible food. If your local farmers understand and follow your national standards, then by all means purchase their food, even though it might not be called "organic".

Compare food value with other financial investments. We ignore the cost of that fancy design magazine, but curse over the price of a block of cheese that will last us several days. We are upset at the cost of feeding our children basic food items but then spend generous amounts on computer games and fancy hair-streaks.

We could get a grip on our priorities and value the foods we buy as investments. We are nourishing a body, supporting a farmer (hopefully an organic one) and looking out for the birds and bees with our well-spent dollar.

Be aware of what you spend money on by checking your grocery print outs from time to time. I was shocked to find that a good chunk of my monthly grocery expense was taken up with snacks to take to work — dried fruit and nuts were darned expensive. I switched to apples and rice chips and saved about thirty dollars a month in that one step.

Don't Waste a Thing

Restaurant chefs should be teaching us how to plan meals. They know when they cook up a batch of food that they will have to invent meals around the leftovers for days to come, and then, unlike many of us, they do it. This idea might be as simple as not taking a big hunk of something out of the freezer when you know you'll be out of the house for the next three nights, but certainly automatically planning soup nights after a meat dinner or learning several good stir fry recipes for leftover cooked veggies is a good thing.

Limit the amount you buy so that the last batch is not begging for airtime in the crisper as the replacement comes in the front door. And don't cook in bulk to save money if you hate leftovers. Put the extras right into marked containers in the freezer and then eat them.

Buy in Bulk

Every time our food is handled for packaging, the price goes up so that the worker can be paid. To measure, fill and label a jar costs the same whether it is a gallon of pickles or just a few grams. That is one of the reasons that large quantities of products are sometimes not much more than the small amounts. It was not really the product in the jar or bag that costs the money, it was the transportation, storage, workers, labels and marketing. And food producers aren't unaware of our habit of running in and grabbing just what we need for the least amount of money. They make a lot more profit selling small amounts twenty times a day than one big one. Our savings are in that bigger size package.

Naturally, we would all be buying large sizes if we had the money, right? But it's frequently impossible to invest in a flat of tomatoes when we haven't paid for our bus pass to get to work. This is where the co-op comes in handy. If you can find a friend or two to share the cost, it gets easier to buy a flat or large package. If you can find five friends and buy the giant size, all the better. It takes very little to start a food co-op. Someone needs the ability to get to a grocery store when there is a good sale on and bring home the largest size they can manage. Everyone else needs to pitch in their portion of costs, and to have lots of small bags and jars on hand for divvying up the abundance. Someone needs a small scale or measuring cups so that flour and grains can be divided fairly. And then you're all off home with sacks of affordable loot. Politics in these groups differ depending on circumstances so things can be as casual or formal as the members desire. And if a group doesn't suit you, start one that does.

Be watchful of someone doing more than their share. They may be good at what they are doing, but be sure to lighten their load or they may back out.

Buying Wholesale

This is a step beyond buying bulk food or large sizes from your grocery store. You can approach wholesalers and distributors and ask their minimum amount for opening an account. Buying this way gives you even better savings because you cut out the middle guy. You do have to come up with a whack of dough to get started, and the more you buy, the greater the responsibility of collecting funds from a larger number of people. You also need a reasonable sized space to unload and distribute this food from, and the greater issue of keeping insects at bay and

Get in the good habit of saving paper and plastic bags, yogurt containers and large jars to be ready for your first food division. Discuss the breakdown of everyone's duties. If someone follows sale ads at night, and someone has the wheels to pick up flats, and someone else looks after the kids while the food is being broken up, and someone figures out each share, individual tasks are small and manageable. Looking at the soft spots of some local cooperatives, it might be a good idea to write some consequences into your job list. Then, if someone consistently lets you down, they'll understand that they will be paying more for their share for the inconvenience.

worrying about what to do with a case of frozen fish when the power goes out. Still, this system works.

Make Your Own

This paragraph could also be called "learn to cook." Making a big vat of soup with left over veggies, knowing how to chop all the vegetable ends into a wok for stir fry, making potato pancakes from a sprouting bag of spuds are all excellent ways to pull potential compost fodder back from the brink.

▬ Basic soup-making skills ▬

Making soup feels mysterious until about, oh, the first time we try it. Then a whole world opens up. I think the first humans that created a cooking pot probably found great satisfaction in tossing in all sorts of roots, leaves and perhaps critter bits, and watching it all swirl and blend into a heart warming, belly soothing mess.

If you're not careful, when you look in good cookbooks for soup recipes, they will discuss stocks and broths and filtering all the big bits out. Heck. The big bits are the best part! Let's look at a couple of foolproof recipes. Try at least one of them out, but if you like it, build from there.

▬ Potato Leek Soup ▬
(or leek potato soup, depending on what you have more of)

This is a rib sticking soup, very easy and good to sharpen your teeth on. Leeks are expensive when they're not in season, so only bother making this as a winter meal if you can get these in the sale bin, or better yet, grow your own leeks.

You'll need: Some leeks, say, three small (as wide as your thumb) or two big (as wide as the narrow part of a baseball bat) or more or less. No problem. And you'll need some potatoes, any white fleshed type, equaling about three fists worth. Or more, or less, of the above. See? It's easy.

Some butter or olive oil, a couple of cups of water, salt and pepper. Cream, milk and cheese and garlic are optional.

Do this: Bring out your biggest, thickest saucepan and pour enough oil, or melt enough butter to coat the bottom of the pot well.

Cut the dirtiest part off the leek root, and the mangiest part of the green leek tops off and put them in the compost. Cut away the toughest looking, discolored or ratty dark green parts. Use your own discretion. You can cook the ratty stuff too, if you don't mind the looks of it, but the dense green leaves at the top are chewy, even when cooked. Slice the remaining stalks thin, so they'll cook faster, and put the rounds into a colander or sieve.

Wave the colander full of leek rounds under the cold water tap. Leeks often have soil pushed up around them to keep the stalk white, which means the dirt can be ingrained right into the middle portions, so rinse them carefully.

Toss them into the soup pot and cook them in the butter on medium heat for about ten minutes. Add a bit more oil or butter if need be, and turn the heat down if they are turning brown. Don't go too far away from the action.

After about ten minutes, when your leek is limp (don't worry, for once that's a good thing), pour in a cup of water and put a lid on the pot. Cook that for ten minutes as well, and meanwhile, cut your potatoes up into any cook-able, same-size pieces, and toss these into the soup pot. Pour in a cup or so more water to cover and put the lid back on. Now you can relax a bit as the potatoes slowly cook. Take a peek now and then and watch them gently simmer. It will look like grey glop at this point, and that's alright.

Test the potatoes with a fork after about half an hour. Are they soft? Starting to fall apart?

Good!

If you have a blending wand, pull it out now, blow the dust off it, and push it into the soup. It will start grinding up the potatoes and making a creamy purée. How much you blend it is totally up to you. You could mash it with a potato masher, too, or toss it into the blender. Or you could leave the whole works and eat it the way it is.

If your soup now looks quite a bit like wallpaper paste, good for you! You're almost up to the finish line now.

If you taste your soup now, you'll find it amazingly
bland and gruel-ish. Grate some cheddar cheese into it until
you can see a faint change in the shade. Put your pot over
low heat, taste it, and start adding salt and pepper until it
has a richer taste. Cheese contains salt, so adding more of
that can help. Add half a cup or so (or more or less) of milk
or cream now. Stir this all together for a few minutes to let
it mingle. If the soup seems too thin, slowly raise the temperature and cook off some of the water. If it seems too
thick, slowly add some water or milk, stirring gently all the
while, till the thickness suits you. Taste it one more time,
and serve.

Other options: Chop in green onions at the last minute,
or chopped cooked ham, or squish in some garlic, or throw
in some croutons. Great with crusty bread on a winter night.

Basic Chicken Soup

Organic chicken is expensive, but since I insist on buying
local farm chickens that ran around outside eating good
food, this restricts me to buying stewing fowl, which are
birds that have put in their time producing eggs, and who
the farmer might decide not to pay to be on vacation all
winter. These old chooks are tough as nails to eat, but don't
taste of cardboard like their factory raised cousins. They are
also very affordable, and if we follow our rule of eating way
less meat, we can decide to really enjoy every bit of these
precious little critters. Use a bag of backs and necks if you
are using the conventional method of shopping.

Coat the bottom of your biggest cooking pot with lots
of oil, and chop any size onion and any amount of celery
into it to start cooking. Section your little beastie as best
you can, and toss the pieces in. Flip them around to turn a
bit brown all over. When everything is looking a bit toasty in
there, pour enough water in to half drown the chicken, and
smack the lid on and turn the heat down. It takes a loooong
time to encourage a stewing hen to fall apart so give it at
least an hour and a half. Check the water level occasionally
to make sure it is not boiling dry. Test the chicken now and
then, not with a calculus quiz (which would be totally unfair

to give a chicken, especially when dead) but by lifting out a piece and seeing if the meat will shred off the bone easily.

When it does, lift all the pieces out onto a big plate. While those pieces are cooling, chop carrots and potatoes (Any amount! Don't you love these recipes?) into the cooking water and by the time you have finished that, the chicken will be cool enough to tear the meat off of. Return this to the pot, and let everyone cook together until the potatoes are soft. Add salt, pepper and garlic to taste.

This is ready to eat now, or you can fancy it up. Add a tin of tomatoes, add macaroni noodles, or raw or cooked rice. Cooked or raw mushrooms. Lots of garlic. Thyme and oregano, or parsley. Add cream or milk, or thicken it with a bit of flour mixed with cold water, blended well, and stirred in very slowly. And if you want to get really fancy, and have done the flour and water thing, heat some oil or butter in a little frying pan and add some curry paste with or without *garam masala*, or with extra cumin. When this has spattered around in the pan a moment, stir it into your chicken veggie mix, and cook it down till the whole thing thickens a bit. You can pour this over rice as a faux curry.

▬ Basic stir fry skills ▬▬▬▬▬▬▬▬

Here's another basic recipe that can be twisted in a dozen ways and still deliver the goods. You'll need a wok or frying pan, and some oil. Olive or canola oil is fine, peanut oil is good. Put the wok and oil on medium high heat and start chopping. Cut a yellow onion of any size, and cut celery on an angle to make the surface area bigger. While that cooks, throw in a big spoonful of black bean sauce and slice in the carrots, broccoli and/or cauliflower. Things that cook more quickly go in later in the game. Cut up some cabbage, small toothpicks of sweet potato, zucchini, peas and beans, mushrooms and peppers, and then toss it all in. Dribble in some soya sauce and sesame oil if you have it. Last, toss in sliced lettuce or chard and green onions, garlic, and last and most surprisingly of all, break an egg on the lip of your pan and stir that in. Let it all cook for several more minutes. You can add cooked rice, hot sauce, peanut sauce or Asian noodles to this to bulk it out, or just eat it as is. Tasty in whatever form, but very dependant on a good veggie garden!

Working for Your Food: Long-term or Day Trades

If you're having one of those weeks (you know the kind), and you just need someone to say "yes" to you, just once, ask any farmer if they need help. Farming is hard work. But the problem for farmers is that it is generally so low-profit, that every penny given to the necessary employees is a penny less for the farmer to manage through a slow period or a bad crop. And farmers can't use just anybody. They need someone who can work alone at a seemingly thankless task for many hours — in the rain. Or sun. And without whining endlessly about it later. But if you are a patient person with a good back and your own fertile imagination to amuse you, approach your closest farm and ask if you can work for some food. You might even want to make a list of your skills. Can you mend a fence, sort beans, fix a roof, turn soil for hours? Maybe your local farmer will give you a full trade for hours worked, or maybe a discount. Don't forget you're going to learn about food growing by making this deal, as well as developing good pectorals. It's an excellent time to learn some good yoga stretches, though. A day of bending is torture for those who are out of shape.

Marry a Farmer

Or hey, it's modern times. You could just sleep with a farmer. Although this is a clever way to get close to a food supply, farming is work intensive and you may still be expected to sing for your supper. *Singing* in this case may translate as fence mending, bean sorting, roof repair and soil turning, but there might be fun parts later in the day. That is, if you're not too tired.

More Trade for Food

If you're city bound, you might want to offer to help out at your local health food store in exchange for trades or discounts. You could offer everything from improving their logo, picking up items, doing packaging, and splitting in the back, or pricing. My local food co-op owner, Jean, makes trades like this occasionally, but she finds that sometimes her workers are so slow to pick up a good rhythm at their new tasks that she can usually do the job faster herself. Take into account that you need to offer quality time and effort to make these trades worth it.

Community Supported Agriculture

Ask around to see if there are any Community Supported Agriculture or CSA farms in your community. These farms work with less risk because people pay up front for their summer's food, so the farmer can relax and get on with the task of good food growing instead of figuring out where to sell it every week. CSA growers need help with harvesting, cleaning and box packing and a friend of mine would put in a hard day's work and be happy to go home with a big box of healthy grub.

An interesting fact that came up during a casual food security scan in our rural community was that it would not typically be our low wage earners who would get into trouble during an emergency. They were used to looking after their problems and frequently had a good veggie garden and a full larder, a woodstove and even a back up outhouse. It was our more well-off friends who would be in a fix, with their monster homes which would now be impossible to heat, quickly defrosting freezers and no year-round garden. (Hmmmmm…)

Have Your Own Garden

I hear the complaint that it is not worth having a veggie garden because of the small percentage of purchased foods it would displace, and being me, I always beg to differ.

My own pickings may feel meager sometimes, but when I add up the dinners I will be enjoying, things start to make sense. One dozen leeks and four potato plants is four big winter pots of potato leek soup. Three big squash is six dinners with squash on the side plus three pots of yummy soup with the leftovers. One jar of hard won soup beans is still ten good meals. You stop counting at some point and just start planting.

Food for Free

The organic co-op I visit has a "Free" shelf. Jean moves foods into place when they develop a little softness or a blemish. Most of us who use it are quite respectful about dipping into it, lest we scoop more than our share, leaving none for someone who really needs a break. But the next step after the "Free" bin is the compost heap, and in that case, I, for one, who hate to see good food wasted, will then load up. When I see a bag of mushrooms sitting there, I bring it home and slice them into my food dehydrator to dry for winter dinners. The odd tray of tomatoes is quickly converted to sauce, with anything else lying in the garden or fridge, and poured over pasta or thrown into the freezer. One year when Jean was pulling her hair about tossing bruised tomatoes out, I took them home, cut out the bad parts, dried the sliced tomatoes and packed them in oil for Christmas presents.

Gleaning

Sometimes, if we put our feelers out, we find there is food in our community that no one can handle. When the people up the road get their apple trees destroyed by bears, I pick up the leftovers and make apple butter in the communal juicer. Rural folk have trouble giving apples away, so it's good to have a plan. I'm looking for more rose hip recipes because it's almost time to harvest them. Many people haven't got a clue what to do with a laden grape vine. Throw them (on the branch and still with seeds in) into a borrowed extractor/juicer, with some apples if you have them, add a bit of sweetener to the basin towards the end and pour the juice off into jars. You can pop these jars into the canner, or you can freeze them. Or if the grapes are seedless, learn to make raisins.

Up on the verge in the next town, some giant walnut trees grow and sometimes in autumn, you'll see people with bags picking up the fallen nuts and taking them home to clean and dry. The back roads are lined with berry pickers come blackberry season around here. Those in the know haunt the dripping forests in search of the many mushrooms that poke out of the soft moss, and those who fish, fish.

In the cities, churches and community groups support food banks and lunch programs, so that those in need can get a warm, full tummy. Grocery stores put boxes of produce outside in the back alley in our town, supposedly for folks to feed their rabbits but I have visited more than one friend who has chopped the bad bits out of this food and made a casserole. Rabbits — let them eat grass!

Things to Try

- Offer to be the one in your community to raise funds to purchase a juicer/extractor and pressure canner for a group to use.
- Find a couple of people nearby who would buy large sizes of flour or flats of canned tomato to share with you.
- Call the closest food wholesaler in your phonebook and ask what it would take to begin a co-op.
- Try to think of *free* foods that you might be ignoring.

Resources

Hennessey, David. "How to Buy Organic Food Inexpensively." davidhennessey.ca/buyorganicfood.htm. (2006).
A downloadable e-book by British Columbia writer on how to eat healthy, save your pocketbook, and the planet. Lots of ideas and updates are available to purchasers.

"A Report Card for the EPA: Successes and Failures in Implementing the Food Quality Protection Act," Consumers Union of United States, Inc, February 2001, consumersunion.org/pdf/fqpa/ReportCard_final.pdf.

CHAPTER 4

Getting Symbiotic With Your Garden

The planet is already sinking under the weight of food gardening books, so this chapter was written to light up some unspoken truths for those who haven't broken ground yet, and to add some brain compost for those who have.

In terms of food security, walking outside your door into a landscape full of fresh groceries is your number one bet. But where should you start? There are a million and one combinations of what could possibly be contained in a vegetable garden. Although we think we are eating the same foods as the next guy, like snowflakes, no two gardens are exactly alike. Their contents are formed by our food preferences, our available time, garden microclimates, and even the shape of our own bodies. People with big arms "double dig" and those with little arms tend to throw mulch on top. People with lots of time have order and tidiness, and busy folk have delightful chaos. But the other difference in our food gardens is our real purpose in having one. We all say we want food from our food gardens, but there is a huge difference between the person hoping for some tomatoes to show off, and someone who is desperate to feed their little ones for much of the year. The latter knows they cannot waste an inch or a minute. Practicality and wise moves are the theme of the focused gardener. No showy pretensions here. Needs get shaved down to the bare bones — good soil, lots of biodiversity, strong observational skills, careful timing and intelligent use of space. It's hard to buy any of the above, but they can all be achieved with time and guilt free experimentation.

Since there is lots of information out there on soil building, lets take a peek at the lesser-discussed issue of biodiversity in our yards. It's hard to do all the work alone in our gardens, so we need to call in help. Cheap help is good, free help is best. Who can pick those little bugs off our plants, how can we keep our lettuce plants lush, how can we get more air to our plant roots without all the extra work? Well, it just so happens that the more diverse our garden is, the more help will magically appear to assist us. If we leave wild edges of native plants around our garden, foraging birds and pollinating insects who recognize these plants will stay nearby. If we plant highly scented herbs like sage and fever-few amongst our special plants, hungry bugs will get the scent mixed up and get lost in the foliage. If we use half-digested nutrients like seaweed, shells and manure on our gardens, something is bound to appreciate the meal, and as our varied upper layer breaks down, worms will be happy to digest it and turn it into castings inside their precious little air tunnels.

A well mixed garden means that spike rooted plants like comfrey and dandelion are bringing up nutrients for more shallow rooted plants, and that sun loving plants are offering respite to the shade lovers behind them. The advantage to you, besides avoiding crop failure by always having something that will get through a strange weather system, is a nice healthy balance of energy between your plants and your insect life. And the way to accomplish all this diversity stuff is to basically turn your hard earned common sense on its head and to begin being a bit freer in your garden.

We tend to plant gardens in terms of their perceived use, such as a veggie garden here, flowers there and grass over there when it may actually be a better idea to plant things where they are best suited, and not worry too much about what the heck they are supposed to be doing for human design concepts. As a matter of fact, the more species you can cram into an appropriate spot, the better. As long as your dry shade, or full sun, or forest edge plants are all where they should be, it won't matter if they are culinary herb, pretty shrub or native plant. In fact, like that dinner party you threw where all the *wrong* people showed up, and it was a smash hit regardless, loosen up with how you arrange your plants, and cram in all the different elements you can. And then do that with your life.

Observational Skills: What's That All About?

Humans have a lot of strange ideas in their heads about what plants really want. Sometimes using good observation can take you to new places. The essay below illustrates where observation can win over habit, but you may just think I'm lazy...

Non-Competitive Gardening or the Anti-Olympian Grower (Lower, Slower, Maybe Next Year)

A funny thing happened when I gave up trying to be a good gardener. Not that I had ever been one. I had never had a garden that people entered and oo-ed and ah-ed at. I was too practical to worry about beautiful placements and shading my mauves perfectly. But I would madly pull out clumps of weeds and prepare window boxes and have some pretty flowers that looked just so from the road, and would hope that everything grew big, because big was good. And I used to clean up my garden in winter and try to shape my bushes and trees so that they looked pleasant or something. I would try for a semblance of normalcy amongst the chaos of my natural gardening style. And then I had one of those crazy epiphanies one day. I was standing on a path with a small hawthorne tree in my hands, wondering where to plant yet another one. My garden buddy Val had dug this little shoot up and given it to me, but crawling feelings were wrapping themselves around my planting arm. I thought, and I can hear it now, "Someone will think I'm crazy if they see I have two hawthorne trees in this little side garden." Yes, imagine! What would people think if they saw me, alone in the bush on the side of Mount Elphinstone, with *two haws* growing lustily away? And all those weeds and untied vines and crazy herbs that no one uses anymore? *What would people think?*

I realized that the stress of having a garden that others would approve of was taking more energy than it took to support and enable a truly healthy garden. It was at that moment I began to change my ways. I started worrying about the needs of individual plants instead of how they looked. I started making sure the habitat for birds and bees made sense to them even though it meant letting the pearly everlasting grow all through my best garden bed. I let things grow in mixed clumps with whoever they happened to go to seed with. I let huge dandelions grow amidst the rare Chinese medicinals to see if it bothered them at all. I stopped pruning a lot of things that were growing into the paths because after all, a garden is for plants, and the people can just duck and watch their heads. I put showy, beautiful things I had been fussing over behind the fence because they actually wanted to be in the shade.

And then a crazy thing started happening — the plants grew in more lush and bigger than ever, now that my fat ego was out of the way, and the gardens vibrated with insects and energy. People started to ooh and ah.

Things do get messy, though. I mulch with anything I can get my hands on, which means there are piles of cardboard and wood chips all over the place. But those mulched areas need much less in the way of weeding and watering. There are piles of sawdust right along the pathway, which is unattractive, but easy to access. Snake houses are close to the gardens, which gives certain visitors the willies, yet the slug-eating garter snakes are happy. Location, location, location.

I leave my hoses out now, because real gardens have hoses in them. My little apple tree has branches hanging right onto the ground, which I refuse to tend, and the tree is covered with apples each year despite my lack of care. And in late summer I actually permit some plants to do what they do naturally during a late summer drought — curl up and die — only to return with great zeal the next spring.

It did occur to me that I might just be terribly lazy, and I also realized that humans feel largely unneeded when plants grow boisterously and joyfully without them. Sometimes I go out and meddle just for the hell of it. It keeps me busy, and more importantly it keeps me in a place full of love and health, with a lot less stress.

Where to Start?

It helps, while a garden is rolling into good health, to figure out what you actually want from it. Since a garden relationship is completely symbiotic (it supports you and you support it. It feeds you and you feed it. It loves you and you love it.) you have to start that wheel turning by figuring out your utmost desires and getting them happening.

What Do You Eat?

Think up that fantasy garden and begin filling in your dietary needs. Here are a few ideas to get you started.

Breakfast: Fried potatoes, carrots, parsnips or squash; eggs, veggie quiche; fresh fruit, jam.

Lunch: Berries including tree fruit with yoghurt; bean dishes; hot and cold salads (such as hot potato salad); herbal tea.

Dinner: Squash soups; bean dishes; combo tomato sauces from the garden; salads; stir fry greens; squash flowers with cheese; potato leek soup; cordial; culinary herbs.

That Little Timing Thing

Once a garden gets going, it rolls around in predictable cycles that you can plan your lunch around. There are overlaps and exceptions to the rule, but basically, your list of available foods looks like this.

Winter

From January through March, nearly all that is edible out there is underground. Tuberous plants have spent the summer and late fall turning sunlight into carbohydrates that they can use later on next year's growth, and have repaired underground for the duration. They are easy pickings if you remember where your rows are. Lift off your mulch, and dig up potatoes (leave the smalls to re-sprout in spring for your next generation), parsnips, carrots, beets, sunchokes, Chinese artichoke, turnip and rutabaga. Chop off the sprouting top, rinse the soil off, and load them into a bucket for the house. There will still be some leafy greens in the form of collards, kale, chard, dandelion and plantain, garlic greens and mache (a leafy green). Winter annuals that you planted last summer, like leeks and cabbage, are now ready.

Starting in late February, the lack of hard frost will release a lot of leafy greens to start afresh. If you let your fall plants go to seed by themselves, you'll see the babies springing forth as soon as it is warm enough. Unlike your little trays of seedlings inside, these will pick their own date to be born, and will fly out of the soil completely unaided by you, making you wonder what the heck you are doing inside with your sickly, dependant little seedlings. At any rate, pinch off individual leaves of these early spring plants, or snip the plant off at the root. If you leave the root in, you'll get a second bit of growth.

How to Change the Seasons to Match Your Zone

Keep in mind that this list was developed for the coastal 49th parallel. If you live north or south of this, tilt this page accordingly until the harvest dates slide onto the right part of the page. Usually, because weather is unpredictable anyway, it is best to tilt it by one month. If you live on the other side of those big mountains, better to use a proper planting chart that shows your particular zone.

Spring

By April, many of your tuberous plants will be beginning the hard work of re-growing their tops so that they can go to seed. This takes — you guessed it — the same carbohydrates it takes you to do hard work, and the tubers of many plants will start to digest themselves as they send out a strong seed head. Watch for a thick central stalk appearing from your parsnips and carrots. Let at least one of them continue its work while you quickly eat the rest. If you leave them too long, you'll have forty seven million seeds, and a handful of shrunken roots.

The tension mounts in May, as the purple sprouting broccoli is covered in tasty knobs, the greens really are at their best, and the salmonberries are out. But June is when the berry season truly gets underway. Strawberries are the first to ripen, and please try to keep your mitts to yourself until the little tip on the bottom of the berry is just red — true ambrosia. You will never go back to those plastic store-bought things again. And the dual-season raspberries will be pumping out their first crop. June is also time for little pea pods to get big enough to strip off the vine and eat, the tea herbs are hitting their stride, and watch those bamboo shoots so you can nip them off for dinner. The rhubarb is really a good size by now and the cherries are out. June is the time that the heat-loving annuals get their grip into the planet and begin a burst of energy.

Summer

In July there's a long rush of madness as everything happens at once. The last of the strawberries coincide with the tay and logan berries and boysenberries needing desperately to be picked. The peas are starting to slow down just as the bush beans begin to put out their tender little young. The first of the garlic are ready to pull, and baby potatoes are a decent size for steaming in butter. And you might as well eat all those extra squash flowers.

By August, oh dear, I seem to recall something about reading a murder mystery in the hammock. And yet, how can one sit down when the fruit has begun to come in? Peaches and pears, early apples, all need picking and preparing in chutneys and pies and bags of dried fruit for later. The squash is coming in, with zukes and tomatoes, the last of the garlic and the very first of the grapes, pole beans and corn, all ready at once. And sheesh, isn't this a good time to harvest more herbs to dry for the winter? While you're at it, let beans go to seed so you'll have lots to pack away for soup.

Most of the annual garden mayhem carries right into September, with the addition of the summer squash all needing eating at once. And you might as well fry the last of the squash blossoms since they won't be able to mature fruit at this time of year. Meanwhile, your leafy greens are finally getting the cool moist nights that invigorate you both so much, and your salads are starting to perk up again.

Fall

Oh no! October already! Just when you wanted to lie down, right? And coincidentally so do your plants. But they are producing storage foods just when you need to stock up for winter. Pole beans for drying, grapes for juicing, the rest of the winter squash to bring in, potatoes put away, nuts and apples, green tomato relish to be put up, and some beet greens are still popping up. And speaking of popping up, those leafy greens are still looking great. And by the time the first frosts have hit, those parsnips and carrots will have sweetened up for harvest...and there we go again!

Map of Garden Food Availability

January

Indoor (winter storage): Squash, garlic, dried beans and peas; other dried and home canned foods; teas, and grains. Bean sprouts and other sprouts (available year-round).

Outdoor: Veggies such as cabbage and leeks (holding on); potatoes, parsnips, sunchokes, carrots, and beets (under mulch).

February

Indoor: Same as above.

Outdoor: Same as above. New and re-sprouting greens such as sorrel, welsh onion, corn salad, collards, kale, chard, chickweed, and cleavers, plus you'll still have some Brussels sprouts, leeks and cabbage at their peak.

March

Indoor: Same as above.

Outdoor: Under mulch — eat tubers soon as they will decrease in size if allowed to grow new tops. Greens doing well.

April

All greens doing well.

May

Greens, purple sprouted broccoli, asparagus, bok choy, garlic greens, and green onions.

A Long and Quite Thrilling List of Edible Greens

Asian greens
Chard
Chives
Kale
Leaf celery
Lettuce
Mache
Miner's lettuce
Mustard leaves
Nasturtium leaves
Purple sprouting broccoli
Sorrel (including the little wild ones and wood sorrel)
Spinach
Violet leaves and flowers
Welsh onions

June

Strawberries, raspberries, salmonberries, peas, cauliflower, lettuce, tea herbs, cole flowers, daylily flowers, bamboo shoots, fava beans, rhubarb, ox eye daisy, cherries, chives, early garlic, and very early potatoes.

July

As in June, plus apples, apricots, artichokes, onions, bush beans, favas, squash flowers, raspberries, boysenberries, garlic, potatoes, and onions.

August
Blueberries, beans, broccoli, plus small squash, tomatoes, eggplant, pears, apples, peaches, pole beans, and grapes, and possibly some of the plants listed below.

September
Blackberries, grapes and corn, sunchokes and hazelnuts, and some of the October list will be also ready.

October
Late apples, pumpkins, winter squash, last of beans, carrots, beets, potatoes, and broccoli. Apply mulch.

November
Parsnips after first frost. Cabbage, beets, and carrots. Winter greens such as sorrel, welsh onion, corn salad, collards, kale, and Swiss chard might still be good.

December
Indoor: All winter storage foods. See January's list.
Outdoor: Under mulch.

Now that we're super clear on how our ability to observe cycles will affect our garden choices, we'll see that timing is pretty crucial to the whole thing. We need to get our seeds or small plants in on time, but better yet, it is important to have an area in the garden prepped and ready for these little babes. This is a step that is often overlooked. This whole cycle/timing thing in the garden can sometimes be pretty overwhelming, but fortunately, we have access to some simple charts that will tell us exactly what we should be doing in our growing zones. I lose track of time like politicians lose votes, but when I stop dead and wonder what the heck I should be doing right about now, I pull out my planting chart and am always assured that there is something that can be started by seed right now, and that little nap in the hammock will just have to wait. Garden prepping is another matter.

Stepping out into your garden with a brand new flat of winter cabbage and finding that you actually need to spend time pulling out old plants and digging in a little bit of nutrition can take all the wind out of you. Best to keep the garden mulched at all times, because then you know that the soil underneath is cool, soft and damp. It means always having some soil amendment tucked away for this occasion such as a bag of alfalfa pellets, some seaweed and a steaming pile of compost. Timing is something you stumble over and then eventually just climb into like an old gardening shirt.

Use Space Well

Good use of space, ah yes. We were still talking about the things that help us be good gardeners. Using space well is a number one skill. You'll learn a bit more about it in the next chapter. The basics of space use are:

1. Plants that need full sun have it, the rest crouch around in the fringe areas.
2. Use lateral space well.
3. Don't waste good gardening space on inanimate objects.
4. Remove spent plants and put in new ones right away.

Feeding the Garden

Feeding the garden really is a symbiotic relationship. Here are some quick tips for keeping your soil nutrient-rich for your plants' benefit, so they can feed you better:

1. Lay a mulch on the soil as often as you can. That usually means leaves in the fall, seaweed when the winds blow a batch up to shore, manure when a nice person loans you a truck, and compost when the box is full.
2. Manure tea is easy to apply if you can get your hands on a food grade plastic barrel or an old tub. Toss your weeds and seaweed into it and use the rich sludge that forms, diluted with water and with one hand over your nose. Use this on everything, but in particular your garden plants. They will love you for it!
3. Plant legumes such as bush beans throughout your garden and let them stay and break down after harvest is over so that their nitrogen rich roots can dissolve on the spot.

Like yourself, a garden should be fed slowly but surely. A rich mulch takes care of that, by slowly rotting down to feed the soil

and organisms, and by attracting worms to its cool, moist under-
side so they can feed off it in safety. Bursts of nutrients for annual
plants hitting their stride in early summer can be supplied with a
bucket of manure tea, given as often as you wish.

Getting There From Here

1. If you haven't got a food garden yet, make a list of all the advantages that access to fresh food would bring you. Begin to
   plan how you can either convert your lawn or find a shared
   space.
2. Make a list of all your resistances to growing food (e.g., too
   difficult, you're too lazy, you have physical problems or no
   time). Then, look at each point and think hard about what
   could happen to make your resistance less strong. An example would be that if you feel gardening would make you
   feel cold from being outside in poor weather, then search out
   some warm clothes and gloves that can live near the back
   door to make running outside in the cold easier. If you suspect
   it's laziness, offer yourself a reward, or garden with a person
   you love being around.
3. If you do have a garden, make a list of all the ways you could
   increase the amount of food products that you could be gleaning, and for more of the year.

Resources

Websites

West Coast Seeds' catalogue has fabulous garden tips on how to
start and grow most veggies and best of all, a one-page planting
chart that should be on the front of every refrigerator for when
we wonder what we could possibly be doing out there in the garden. Visit westcoastseeds.com/catalogue to request a catalogue.

Johnny's Selected Seeds is a US employee-owned company.
Their catalogue gets rave reviews for its great information and
resources, as well as the fine seeds. Although this is an East Coast
source for seeds, the information can be used with a little adjust-
ment for areas with earlier springs and longer falls. Visit johnny
seeds.com/catalog/CMCatalog.aspx to request a catalogue.

Books

Bartholomew, Mel. *Square Foot Gardening: A New Way to*

Garden in Less Space with Less Work. New York, NY: Rodale Press, 2005.

Viewed as a cult classic, likely because working one foot at a time is non-threatening. This method creates order from suspected chaos.

Elliott, Carl W, Rob Peterson, and Megan Ernst. *The Maritime Northwest Garden Guide: Planning Calendar for Year-Round Organic Gardening* Seattle: Seattle Tilth, 1998.

Maritime Northwest Climate zone map, month by month gardening help, organic help for plant disease, garden season extending tips and lots more.

Gilkeson, Linda. *Year-Around Harvest: Winter Gardening on the Coast* (self-published, 2005).

This 68-page manual includes detailed information on over twenty kinds of winter hardy vegetables such as what to grow, when to plant and chapters on curing and storing fresh fruit and vegetables, managing common pests organically and saving seeds. Wow! To order a copy, visit the website saltspring seeds.com/catalog/books.cfm.

Jason, Dan. *Greening the Garden, A Guide to Sustainable Growing*, Gabriola Island: New Society Publishers, 1991. (Out of print)

What new growers need to introduce them to rarely used but important food crops, and how to use them in the kitchen.

Wheeler, Robin. *Gardening for the Faint of Heart*. New Catalyst Books (2008).

A vastly expanded version of this chapter, with chapters on shade growing, greenhouse use, garden planning, edible landscaping and lots more.

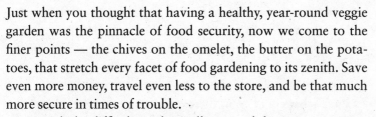

CHAPTER 5

Maximizing
the Harvest

Just when you thought that having a healthy, year-round veggie garden was the pinnacle of food security, now we come to the finer points — the chives on the omelet, the butter on the potatoes, that stretch every facet of food gardening to its zenith. Save even more money, travel even less to the store, and be that much more secure in times of trouble. ·

It might be difficult to physically expand the space you grow food in, but there are plenty of ways to extend the use of what is there. Pick one method and focus, or use them all.

Carefully Choose What You Put in Your Garden

Let's start at the outer edges of your land capacity. We'll imagine that our yard is eighty feet by one-hundred feet. Where is all that precious space you thought you had to grow food in? Problem is, it might be taken up with those seemingly mandatory rhododendrons, lawns (so useful in an emergency), dahlia beds, and dog houses. And then there is that patch under the cedar tree where nothing grows. Now what?

My first suggestion would be to do a quick walk-around and make a list of all the things you can actually eat. The bamboo is good for a few shoots next spring, not a lot, but better than the dahlia bed in terms of snacking. The salal patch is a no care berry source. And you may have an existing fruit tree or vegetable patch. Now is the time to visit the chapters on edible flowers and eating your weeds.

Drag a chair out to your garden space, have a seat, and think about maximizing food units. Many people don't bother growing potatoes because they are so affordable and accessible in the store, but in a pinch, a potato is an energy unit that can be plucked out of the ground several months of the year. It's easy to cook and is appreciated by most people. Squash plants take up space and are not to everyone's taste, but the fruit is edible from the time it appears on the plant, is nutritious and it can grow quite huge. Once harvested, winter squash will keep for a good six months on a shelf in the hallway. Tomatoes could be canned or dried for use over the coming months or even years; while berries will keep as jam or wine. Once you get in the cycle of growing and preserving foods, this is going to start to feel very good.

Most gardens are full of flowers and shrubs, and there seems to be no room for more fruit trees or berry bushes, but you can begin by carefully digging out plants you don't have an affinity for or that don't do well in your garden, and offering them to a kind soul who will tend them. Then analyze that new space and imagine what could go in there. A five way dwarf apple tree, or maybe a grape vine...

Use Space Well

Fences are not just big walls we put up for some privacy from the people next door; they are places to hang food. Yes, you can train grapes, squash plants (in netting baskets), pole beans, peas and indeterminate tomatoes. You can tie berries to fences and espalier fruit trees along them. Fences and walls reflect back heat and light, break the force of the wind and cause a little microclimate at their base where the soil is shaded and where the dew and rain run down and keep the soil moist. You might want to put in a fence or two just to improve your gardening choices.

Use light well: For those gardens with pockets of shade and sun, remember to save your precious sunlight for those plants that absolutely need it like tomatoes, eggplants, peppers and squash. Potatoes, leafy greens and berries will do just fine in four to six hours of sun a day so choose your dingier sites with this in mind.

Interplant: Tuck bush beans into small spaces, place bits of netting for short rows of peas, and don't be afraid to plant kale and cabbage between those silly, inedible flowers. Chives, tea plants like lemon balm and monarda, and surprises like leaf celery can all be planted wherever there is space between existing plants.

Learn to Eat What is Already in Your Garden

Let's look at some of the veggies in our gardens that we might want to gently exploit to the max.

A friend came back from Africa and told me that the people there had a different angle on the common broccoli plant. They ate the stems and leaves and discarded that silly old flower head. That story made me go back outside and look at my plants again. I realized I had been taught to think that the part that's available in the grocery store is the only part that was edible. We eat kale leaves, and cabbage leaves so why not broccoli leaves? And we could be eating the immature flowering stems and the flowers themselves, and many of the seeds of this family (which includes mustard) are used as a condiment.

And then there is the eating of squash flowers. In a garden hefty with squash plants, all those flowers can certainly add some bulk to the diet. But because we don't want to reduce the number of squash we bring in to eat, it's important to learn about **squash sex** before plucking these off. Once that is done, you will be frying up big yellow blossoms for decades. The first thing we have to do in our sex lesson is learn to tell the girls from the boys.

Boy squash flowers grow on long thin stems that turn immediately into blossoms. Girl flowers have a miniature squash

> The first stages of your edible landscape may look a little odd to the people on your street. Some of us were taught early that it was wrong to stand out in a crowd. Sometimes we feel shy about being the first on our block to put in an obvious anomaly like an edible garden. Those people down the street may call us names, but among them will have to be, "Well Fed" and "Planet Friendly" and "Prepared." When we get razzed by a passing complainer, we have to smile and give them an apple, a peach, or...a raspberry.

right at the base of the flower that will begin to develop once it is fertilized through the flower. Many people run outside, take a good look and say, "Well, I'll be!" when they hear this stunning revelation. So we all know that we need girls and boys and bees for good squash production, but we also know that squash are notoriously bad for arranging their trains to arrive at the same time. Frequently, a flush of males will arrive, look around frantically, and then die a noble death only to be followed days later by a couple of fresh young gals, who then whither quickly into spinsterhood. Alone.

Occasionally, and it seems only to be an accident of fate, a male and female appear at the same time and you can then wait

---

Be Reasonable — Even With Yourself

We don't suddenly turn from casual veggie gardeners to full sustenance farmers in one year. Choosing specific goals and just watching how the rest comes along each year is an easy method for increasing your food independence level.

Here is my own list of goals for food security on my property:

1. *To grow all my own potatoes* — I mastered this the first year, then slipped as I added more gardens.
2. *All my own garlic and culinary herbs* — This one is pretty easy. Once the herbs are in they just need a bit of weeding, and garlic, once planted each year, is pretty low maintenance.
3. *All my own herb teas* — I got this together by the second year and can store enough each winter to last me, and to sell the excess.
4. *All my own squash and beans* — I never have enough of either and am still working on it.
5. *Salads for eight months of the year* — I still buy some lettuce from time to time to add to my stronger, wild greens.
6. *Green onions for eight months of the year* — Good old Welsh onions.
7. *All berries* — I finally have enough for fresh eating for four months of the year (plus lots for jams and pies) and fruit for two months of the year. The apple trees are finally kicking in although not enough for winter storage.
8. *Home preserving* — I am learning a few skills each year and have now canned lots of fruit, and dehydrated some tomatoes and mushrooms, and pressure canned my first salmon and various soups.

Personalizing your own list will give you a yardstick to see how you are doing as far as increasing your food self-sufficiency.

for a bee to do its thing, or practice a little squash artificial insemination, and then WHOMP! That guy is dinner! Eat him up — he's not much good for anything now! Actually, all unattended squash flowers are dinner, as are unmatched ones, as well as males who are closing up during the day in a way that would not permit a bee to enter. Pluck them off at the stem, check for bugs, pull off the green (calyx) and proceed directly to the kitchen. More on this in the chapter on Eating Flowers!

Often overlooked on the squash plant are the small fruit that do not look like they'll mature. Maybe they've been damaged with a tool, and are getting a bit brown, or maybe it's just obvious at the end of the season, that there won't be time to get them to winter storage size. Pull these off the vine and take them into the kitchen. Chop them into a salad or cook and freeze them for next winter's tomato sauce. This works for all squash, including pumpkin, blue hubbard, and butternut. Even though they're tiny, they taste great. Other things you can eat when tiny are beets, potatoes, peas, beans, and carrots. Even green tomatoes! What about really old things that are generally tough and woody? Well, zucchini that's past its prime can be boiled in tomato stew or made into cake. A long slow cooking in fluid will save a few old things from the compost heap.

Use Low-Tech to Stretch Your Season

Centuries ago, humans noticed that plants growing in front of rocks did better than their exposed cousins, and began building stone forms for tender trees and plants to grow inside of. The stone would hold sunlight all day, and would slowly release it at night, giving the plant a bit more time to be warm, and perhaps more importantly, reducing the day-night temperature swing that can be so annoying for a fruiting body. And as soon as humans invented glass, a whole new dimension opened up (literally) as the invention of greenhouses, bell jars, lean-tos and sunrooms added to each end of the growing season. Once you start growing greens under protection, you can get another month in the spring and winter for eating good salads and stir-frys.

My friend Bruce has greenhouses that produce great veggies early in the season, as well as late into the fall. It's always a surprise to see his harvest basket on the kitchen table when we're all struggling with cold spring soils. Eliot Coleman's excellent book, *Four-Season Harvest: Organic Vegetables from Your Home Garden All Year Long* has good instructions for building simple greenhouses with materials from your local home improvement store. This book started Bruce and several of his gardening pals down the path of extended growing seasons for a wider variety of delicious fruits and veggies.

And there's another way to stretch the veggie season. Another observation smart humans made was that certain types of carrot, bean and leek were ready to harvest at a different time of the year. So they might have a leek that was ready in mid-winter and another that would take until early spring to be just right. This would explain all those early and late vegetables in the catalogues. (But hey, a vegetable is never late for dinner!) and buying a package of both an early and late variety is a great idea for getting more out of your growing year.

Don't Waste a Thing

An important component to maximizing garden resources is learning how to prevent waste. We might overlook that single handful of ripe peas or a few green tomatoes as not worthy of dealing with, and that kind of inaction adds up. It is likely that in a busy household, a garden might lose almost half of its value, purely in lost opportunity. We can get into good habits of swooping out there every evening with a basket and picking everything we can, and at least getting it into the refrigerator. In a few days, perhaps there will be enough to make a quick batch of freezer bags up. See *Chapter 6: Storing the Abundance* for tips on freezing and drying garden foods.

Limp and frail lettuces may not look happy in a salad but can be chopped with scissors at the last minute into a stir-fry or fried rice. Handfuls of peas and beans can be put out with dinner in a bowl for munching if they are too small in amount to cook up.

And for those pea and bean vines that never got properly harvested? No worries! Leave them until the pods get leathery, and on a dry day, pick them into a basket. As you keep noticing these too-late for fresh picking specimens, keep stuffing them into your pockets and keep loading that basket. On a dry fall day, separate the peas and beans, then husk them and put the shiny, beautiful seeds into clean jars. These will keep for soups and such for years, or you can just reach into the jar next spring, pull out a handful of seeds and soak them for planting out.

You could also consider passing the basket over the fence to someone who could benefit from it. There are lots of quiet Karma points buried in that useful gesture. And if you have quantities of food you cannot possibly eat or process yourself, call your local community service office and ask if they have a "grow a row" or a food bank that might benefit from the edible loot. And Salvation Armies and churches sometimes have weekly free meals and might accept and incorporate your goodies. Keep it moving if you can. However, food is never wasted. Left to itself, it will merely fall to the ground and become one with it, food for worms and bugs, and compost for next year's new plants.

Tips

1. Buy three new veggies at the grocery or farmers' market that you have never eaten before that might be grown in your garden.
2. Attempt one new area for lateral gardening each year — netting, baskets on a fence or a set of poles.
3. Start a "Goals" list of garden items to shoot for, such as "all my own beans and squash for the year."
4. Analyze your garden for poorly used space that could hold edible plants.
5. Think of an area of your garden that would benefit from a cold frame or lean-to frame greenhouse, and set out a plan to build one.

Resources

Coleman, Eliot. *Four-Season Harvest: Organic Vegetables from Your Home Garden All Year Long.* White River Jct., Vermont: Chelsea Green, 1999.

The primer for long-season food growing, with lots of tips for extending garden seasons.

Couplan, François. *The Encyclopedia of Edible Plants of North America: Nature's Green Feast.* Chicago Illinois: McGraw-Hill Publishing, 1998.

If you are truly curious about all the edible parts of every plant in your environment, save your pennies and buy this book. Know which stems, seeds and flower head, which sap and catkin, can be consumed. This book is one of my top ten picks of all times and I will depend on it in an emergency.

CHAPTER 6

Storing the Garden Abundance (Top Ten Techniques)

An important component of food security is stocking up and having lots more grub than you actually need for daily use. All this extra stuff can be stored away for a winter day, a trucker's strike, or an earthquake (your call) and in the best case scenario, it just sits there until you want it, because that's a healthy way to live. Whether it's an apple, cabbage or a bit of fish, there are specific storage methods for each food type, and we're going to learn some quick concepts on the hows and whys of long term food storage. Our modern tendency is to stick everything in the freezer, but constant power outages in the Lower Mainland of British Columbia in November and December of 2006 taught us that 100% dependence on our freezers can become a huge waste if all that food turns to mush. What would we do in an earthquake? Fortunately, humans have spent the last few thousand years solving food storage problems, so we have lots of wisdom to draw on.

The main issue with food preservation is that it truly is an organism-eat-organism kind of world out there, and if we find a particular type of food nosh-worthy, then there are likely to be several million other critters on the planet that would like to chow down on that food, too. Humans are pretty good at keeping highly visible competitors like rats, mice and raccoons out of their dinner. It's the miniature stuff we can't see that's harder to fight off. There are molds and fungi and bacteria that can enter our food before we store it or after we put it away. They can merely rot our food into mush so it's easier for them to digest (they know they got there first), or they can live and die and get us later with their leftover toxins. Some of them will stink badly and let us know not to eat the food, some are hardly noticeable until we spend the night on the toilet, and some lie in wait, quietly and without fanfare, and then can be fatal. So we have to take this food preservation stuff pretty seriously. Our lives could depend on it.

The techniques outlined below are discussed in greater detail in the books listed in the Resources section at the end of this chapter. It's important, once you understand and want to try a technique, to make sure you are doing a thorough job of it. And with all these techniques, you will want to start with clean food. So unless it's a berry....

Before canning, freezing or brining make sure the food you use is as clean as you can get it under the circumstances. Clean it under running water, cut it on a clean, scrubbed surface, use utensils that have been washed in hot, soapy water, and then sterilize jars in boiling water for ten minutes.

Technique #1 – Leave it Where it Lay

Some of our garden foods are quite content to stay right in the garden, and don't need inside storage at all. Roots and tubers will be fine under a layer of soil and a good mulch right through to early spring, when the earth warms and they decide to grow again. But catch them before that happens and exploit those lovely carbohydrates for yourself, by digging up your beets, carrots, parsnips, potatoes and sunchokes all winter long. If your area experiences heavy winter frosts, it's a good idea to mulch your tubers well with a thick layer of leaves. This will not only preserve them from winter damage, but make them easier to find and dig out, because the mulched soil will not be frozen hard.

Benefits of Leaving Foods in the Ground

Roots and tubers actually keep way better in the garden than they do any other way. A million years of adapting can't be beat. You don't need extra storage space in the house, and no outside power source is needed.

Drawbacks: (I know this one)
You come home on a rainy dark November night...

It's evening and you hang your coat up to dry, put on your big fat knitted socks and get the house nice and warm. You mosey into the kitchen, and while pulling out ingredients, decide to have some potatoes. Oops! Out into the dark rainy night you go, with boots and flashlight, looking for the shovel and then digging at a frozen pile of leaves because your dinner is tucked under there somewhere. And if you didn't stack your mulch well, dinner will have little mice tooth marks all over it, to boot. Oh well.

Technique #2 – Simple Storage

Some foods are quite content with only a little bit of early fussing to sit in the cupboard for months without any further ado. Apples, cabbage, garlic and squash fit into this category. It's important to clean soil and bugs off food first. Below are a few quick tips for each one.

Apples

Some apples keep better than others in storage, and you may have to find out the hard way how long your varieties will keep. Handle them gently so they don't bruise, and lay them carefully in a box or basket in a very cool place like a basement, perhaps in an open mesh container so that the mice can't crawl in for a meal. Don't store apples near other harvest goodies — they emit a gas that promotes sprouting in many other plants.

Cabbage

Leave the stem and roots on, but tear off the first couple of layers of leaf to check for tiny slugs. They would have quite the party on your stored cabbage before you discovered their now giant, heaving bodies where your food used to be. Store your heads of cabbage in a very humid, cool place like an unheated basement or outbuilding. They will keep a long time, maybe months.

Garlic

Leave garlic until the tops are mostly yellow, then, when you predict a stretch of good weather, pull them up, knock the soil off the roots, and leave them out to dry for a few days. Then gently rub the rest of the soil off and chop all but a nub of root and an inch of stem off them. Bring them in and store them like your onions, in any airy, dry place, with enough warmth to keep the humidity from rotting them. If they start to sprout on you in early February, take them outside and split them into cloves, replant them, give them a good mulching, and see if you can get new heads out of them next year.

Onions

When the tops have died down, wait again for a stretch of clear weather and pull them, then place them on the soil. Roll the onions over in the sun for a couple of days, then cut off all but an inch of the dried top and put them in that nice dry spot where the potatoes are, under the deck or in a warm room. They can cure like this for a week or so, and then pack them in a shallow box. The books say to put the box in a cool spot, but I find this too humid, and they start to rot, and now I leave them one layer deep in baskets under the couch. They never go bad on me now and will keep for months. If your onions are pretty tiny when you dig them up, just cure them as usual and plant them out next spring to try again with a little more manure tea and sunshine.

Potatoes

If you decide to store potatoes, wait until the tops have died down and the weather looks like it will be clear for the day. Needing a good rain for some other purpose generally causes clear weather, so wait for it. Next, carefully dig up your whole potato patch. Check each potato for any damage from your digger, because those ones won't keep. Send them right to the kitchen for washing and pick out the little ping-pong size ones for replanting. Leave the rest on the soil surface for several hours, turning them once in a while. Next, lay them in a dry spot out of the sun (under a deck or in the garage) for about ten days. This will *cure* them, but I'm still not sure of what. Next, pack them in paper bags and put them in the back of a dark cupboard.

They'll be dormant for a few months, and will keep easily during this time. If they break dormancy by trying to grow shoots, and you catch them sprouting early enough, you can move them to a cooler spot to slow them down, or else keep them dark enough and wait until March to plant them back out, with the shoots spread out in the soil, and well covered with some soil and mulch. Or you can nick the shoots right out and eat the potato. Just make sure to remove any green skin or flesh. Green potatoes should go right back to the garden for replanting. Eating the green stuff can make you sick.

Squash (Hubbard, Acorn, Pumpkins, Spaghetti or Butternut)

Leave squash on the vine as long as you can stand it. Early October is a good time to start curing them. Cut the stem leaving a handle to that, uh, fruit or vegetable or whatever that is, and leave the squash out there in the autumn sun for a couple of weeks, sitting on a handful of hay or twigs to keep it off the ground. If it rains a lot, or looks like it will freeze hard, bring it in. Handle it gently so that you don't bruise the flesh. Wipe off the soil, dry it off and put it in a south window or other bright warm place and turn it for a couple more weeks. You can leave squash on the windowsill for up to three months. (I know this for sure.) If the windowsill isn't a good spot, carefully put it up on a dry shelf in the kitchen or hall. Don't let your squash touch each other, and if you see rot starting, eat those squash right away. If you see a bit of mold on the skin you can wipe it with a cloth and some vegetable oil, but keep an eye on those ones. Properly cured squash will keep for several months. Yummy!

Benefits to Simple Storage

There's no outside power needed. Food is close at hand, and needs no thawing or digging.

Drawbacks

If you grow lots of food, bringing it all in can take up a lot of space. Twenty squash, boxes of apples and racks of cabbage need a pretty big storage space. Apartment dwellers would be out of luck. Foods need different conditions to exist in, which may be difficult to find (warm/bright or cool/humid).

Technique #3 — Dehydrating

Dehydrating all the water out of something so it can be put on the shelf for a later day must have occurred to humans quite early on.

That chip of mummified root that had fallen by the wayside could merely be thrown back into the cooking pot, and with sufficient time to rehydrate and cook through, had an amazing amount of taste and nutrient content still in it. (I hope this is true every time I throw something mummified into my soup.) We use dried foods all the time in our everyday life — teas, sun dried tomatoes, bullion cubes, rice, beans, and flour are all foods that we add fluid to and heat in some way to make them tasty again. Some, like raisins and fruit leathers, we just eat in the dry state. Food drying is simple, pretty safe and dependable. You don't need fancy equipment, you can make the components you need, and you can start at any time of year, using it on everything from that apple that is thinking about getting soft on the counter, to the celery leaves you're chopping off the stalks, to the carrots you'll never get around to eating before they rot in the crisper. Or that bag of mushrooms you didn't slice into the salad. North Americans are horribly wasteful with food. We could at least put it aside for a rainy day.

Drying basics

- Lots of the bacteria and molds that land on food and help it to break down will only live if there is enough moisture to support them. Since they cannot survive without water, the trick is to get enough water out of a slice of living food so that nothing else will eat it.
- We can then rehydrate it at our leisure.

To dry food, we obviously need some form of rack to lay it on so that air can circulate around both sides of it. This could be a cookie rack, a wire frame, a piece of fabric stretched between wooden blocks or one of those fancy factory made jobs with the plastic trays. If you are using metal, put some fabric over it to keep the food from touching it. And while it is drying, it is still vulnerable to attack by bigger critters like flies and birds, so we need to either protect it with gauze or hide it under a roof of some kind. And since heat is a good prerequisite to drying, we need to arrange either sunlight, space over a woodstove or other existing heat, or to create it ourselves with light bulbs or elements. The faster something dries, the more likely it is to retain its healthful characteristics, but we don't in most cases want to actually begin the cooking process, which can destroy vitamins. So there is a minor balancing act of having just enough heat and moving air to keep a good drying process going on. 110° F or 43° Celsius is suggested as the proper temperature for preserving nutrients. This won't help you much unless you have a good thermometer and a venting system, but experience will help.

An important factor for getting everything in and out of the food dryer in good time is to have all your slices as uniform as possible. My food drying books says this is a must, but my veggies all come in weird shapes and sizes and there are always strange little bits left over. Don't worry. You will soon find there are cold and hot spots in many food dehydrators, especially those that are home-built. You can put your smallest food bits in the cold spot because they will dry faster so will be out at the same time, or just have the small bits all in one clump where you can brush them onto a plate. We can also simply cut all our food as small as the smallest piece. It will all dry quite uniformly, and quite quickly that way.

If we are drying outdoors, we have to pick a spot that gets full sun for as much of the day as possible, when branches and bugs won't fall into it. We could hold some loose fabric over it with stakes, or to increase dehydration, we could suspend an old window over it. Because it likely won't dry in the first day, we have to be prepared to design our drying spot in such a way that it is easy to carry the trays in at night, or to otherwise protect the food from not only dew, but mice and raccoons.

There are different standards as to when we pull food off the line and into the jars and bags. Small chips of vegetables should be quite brittle, while fruits such as apples should be leathery. Greens should be almost crumbly. Test your dried food after it has cooled to be sure you are judging the texture properly.

If you wish to pasteurize your food to make sure unwanted organisms are truly done in, spread your food chips on a cookie sheet and put in an oven at 175° F (or 79° C) for 10 to 15 minutes. This can also be done if you pull out dried food later and are worried that it has been contaminated in some way, or if it is not as dry as you would like. If I think my medicinal herbs or roots are a little too soft in mid-winter, I just heave the bags up onto the high shelf behind the woodstove for a night or two. Then I have to wait for a tall person to come and get them down.

▬ Home Made Bouillon ▬▬▬▬▬▬▬

Dried chips of: carrot, parsley and/or other
preferred herbs, celery leaf, onions and garlic
Nutritional yeast

You can use dried tomato and mushroom as well. Put in blender and grind to a powder. Store in jars and add to soups and stews.

If your foods are absolutely dry, pack your dried food in glass jars and keep them in a cool, dark spot. Check them very soon. If you see signs of moisture in the jars, leave them in a warm spot with the lids off to truly dry out. In my humid area near the ocean, I feel safer storing my dried products in paper bags up high in my cupboards, where they can breathe out any leftover moisture, instead of rotting in it.

Rehydrate by pouring slightly more boiling water than volume of chips in a bowl, and add more water if they are still rubbery. Put carrots, potatoes and other soup ingredients right into the pot and let them cook with your soup or stew until the texture is good.

Benefits of drying:
1. You can use the sun, or stove heat if you are cooking something else, which means the process does not use extra fuel.
2. Equipment can be built at home at low cost.
3. The process is relatively safe.
4. Many food items can be dried, including meats.
5. The food stays relatively nutritious.
6. Tiny amounts can be saved at any time (e.g., sprig of parsley, three potatoes).

Drawbacks
You need a dehydrator that is reasonably close at hand or you will not use it regularly. Food takes time to rehydrate so is not used spontaneously. Texture may be affected by drying.

Obvious things to dry

Soup stock like onions, mushrooms, kale leaves, carrot slices and celery leaves. Herb tea plants, sliced fruit.

Technique #4 — Canning and Pressure Canning

Food goes bad because humans are not the only organism who wants to eat it. The minute something stops living and breathing in a healthy way, all sorts of teeny little critters fall upon it with great excitement, taking what they can out of its tissues, and turning a perfectly nice piece of fish or a pile of beans into a stinking mess in no time. Humans have puzzled over ways to keep food safe from tiny organisms for a long time, and they have discovered that soaking food in various handy condiments and then storing it in crocks and jars could keep lots of little toxic nasties from living long enough to eat their food supply. Seen in this light, it is a wonder that some of these same condiments haven't pickled us. Examples of some of these condiments are sugar (jam), vinegar (pickles), salt (ham), alcohol (my friend Jim's grandma lived to be 93!) and oil (fish). And even with this treatment, some of these foods will still have to be processed in a hot water bath to kill any microbes that managed to hang on so far. This heating also causes a vacuum within the jar that holds that lid on tight and keeps things even safer. After that, the jars can be put away for several years without refrigeration.

> When a recipe says to pack food into sterilized jars, it means jars that have been submerged in boiling water for ten whole minutes. Do this because losing your canned food after all that work is a bummer.

Basic canning methods

The idea of canning is to boil the food long enough to have killed all the basic normal germs. Cook it up with the sugar or vinegar and pack it in jars leaving a finger breadth of air space. Next, run a clean cloth around the top of the jar to make sure it is perfectly smooth for the lid to stick to. Put the flat metal lids carefully on the jars, place the metal rings on without making them too tight, and then place these jars in a big pot of hot water. Make sure the water level is higher than the tops of the jars. Bring the water to a boil and time it from that moment. When the time is up, carefully lift the jars out with tongs and cool them on the counter. One by one, as the jars cool, the lids go *ping* and suck down against the glass, and that means all is well. Jars that do not go *ping* after the contents are cool can be put into the next batch to try over again. Or eat them right away!

Examples of processing times for pint sized jars
Apples: 15 minutes
Berries: 10 minutes
Cherries: 10 minutes
Fruit juice: 5 minutes
Grapes: 15 minutes
Peaches: 20 minutes
Pears: 20 minutes
Tomatoes: 10 minutes

Benefits to canning
Food retains its taste for a long time. It is safe from bugs and mice, which means it can even be stored in a ratty old crawlspace. It's immediately ready to serve with no defrosting or rehydrating required. Equipment for canning is affordable for most households.

Drawbacks to canning
It requires an energy source, and in the case of pressure canning, needs consistent energy for a long period of time. Some equipment is needed such as a canner, special jars and lids as well as preserving condiments like sugar and vinegar, which can change taste and texture drastically. Also, long canning times can reduce vitamin content.

Obvious things to can
Tomato products, applesauce, homemade chutneys and dilly beans.

Pressure canning methods
If a certain food is very acidic or sweet it will keep after canning for a long time without extra care. But certain foods like meats,

soups and non-acidic vegetables that may not benefit from being dunked in vinegar, like potatoes and peas, need further preparation for their long life in a can. They need what's called pressure canning, which refers to cooking in a special canner that can reach a heat of 240° F for 20–80 minutes, so that every existing organism, such as botulism, has waved goodbye to the world. Pressure canners are huge, heavy to lug around, scare the bejusus out of many of us, and need a small book and a bit of practice to use safely. Other than that, I love mine to pieces. I have cans of soup and fish all lined up in my cupboards, and I love them too.

Using a pressure canner

To use a pressure canner, you need to have a lot of prepared food ready to go, and a lot of jars and packing fluid — either the water you cooked in or some vegetable oil. For instance, have all your salmon cut up into fillets to be rolled into a jar, or your soup ready in a big crock to load up. Read all your instructions carefully, rinsing the jars and checking for nicks along the top, and putting the rack in the base of the canner. Fill your jars, fit the two part canning lids, twist them not too tight, and place them in the canner. After adding a few inches of water to the canner, you would put the canner lid on according to instructions, then struggle to get the whole honking works up onto your cooking element. You would turn the heat up high underneath it. You would watch the steam begin to pour out of the valve on the lid (which you have practiced opening and closing beforehand) for a few minutes to ensure the canner is emptying of air, and then you would flick the valve shut and begin watching the pressure gauge rise as the pressure builds inside the canner. When it reaches the correct pressure (generally ten pounds) you would begin adjusting the heat, or the pot, to keep the pressure at ten pounds, and you would remember to write down what time it was when the pressure hit the right spot, so that you could begin timing it. And when the right amount of time had gone by, you would turn off the heat, flick the control valve open with a pot holder, and stand well back as it exhales all that pressurized air. When the gauge hits zero, you would carefully, with the lid shielding you from the hot steam, open the canner and remove the jars. This is just the nutshell version to get you started. Read the book!

Examples of processing times with a pressure canner

Vegetables: Pint jars – 10 pounds pressure

    Beans: 20 minutes

    Carrots and parsnips: 25 minutes

    Mushrooms: 30 minutes

    Potatoes: 35 minutes

    Soup mixtures: 40 minutes

    Squash: 65 minutes

Meats: Pint jars – 10 pounds pressure

    Roast meats: 75 – 80 minutes

    Chicken stew or curry: 65 minutes

    Fish, clams, crab: 90 minutes

    Oysters: 50 minutes

Note: This information was taken from the booklet called *Canning and Cooking the All-American Way* that was provided with the canner manufactured by American Pressure Cookers.

Benefits to pressure canning

Many foods can be kept well for many years without further worry, but with a slow decline in quality. I love being able to come home from work during a power outage and just pour a jar of garden grown soup into a pan on the woodstove. Voila! A tasty dinner bubbling away in minutes. For more about benefits, see *Benefits of canning* above.

Drawbacks

It takes a lot of power to get these babies up to speed, and even more to keep them at pressure for up to ninety minutes, so this would be difficult if we were using an alternate energy source. A camp stove would work, but a campfire or woodstove might be hard to keep well stoked without a bit of experience. This kind of planning and energy use necessitates making large batches so that it's worth your while. Pressure canners are expensive and must be used very carefully. They are heavy to heave around. And how do we know that pressure gauge is accurate? The small print tells us that the gauges should be checked regularly but I have not met anyone who has ever returned theirs for checking. On the other hand, I don't know anyone who has poisoned themselves with their home canned foods.

Obvious things to pressure can

1. All meats and fish.
2. Stews and soups with and without meat.
3. All non-acidic vegetables like potatoes and carrots.

Technique #5 — Packing in Sugar

Sugar is one of those condiments that organisms cannot live in, which should be a pretty interesting signal to us! But we can use that trait in a positive way for preserving foods. The main groups of foods preserved in sugar are the ones that taste best with it — fruit and berries. This also makes these foods more palatable in their later life. It's always a disappointment to try making a jam with what seemed to be very sweet berries, only to find the fruit strangely sour when we try to eat it later.

Benefits of sugar storage

Complements the foods packed in it. Sugar and honey will store for a long time so can be pre-stocked, sugar is affordable in large amounts, honey has trace nutrients and can be used as a medicine.

Drawbacks

It adds to calorie load, which is good in a crisis and bad in every-day life. And "white death" (also known as refined) sugar, well, we won't go into the politics of that.

Obvious things to pack in sugar

Fruit and berries, candied stems of herbs, and flowers for decoration.

Technique #6 — Packing in Vinegar

Does anyone remember Aunt Edna's Christmas pickles? Although the act of pickling a cucumber is something most of us don't bother doing any more, a tasty pickle in some mayo with a bit of salmon, or on the side of a hot cheese sandwich is divine. Vinegar makes an environment too acid for little bugs to live in, and is good, even added in small quantities to foods that don't normally require it, to help things store away for a long time. But vinegar does have a pretty strong taste. One way around reducing the vinegar "nip" without compromising the food safety component is to add more honey to a recipe. It makes richer end product.

Benefits to packing in vinegar

The acid adds a dash to somewhat dull veggies like beans and cucumbers. The technique is not too complicated to do and it is hard to go wrong. Also, food keeps safely in vinegar for some time.

Drawbacks

Good clean vinegar will be hard to find in an emergency so you better stock up beforehand. It certainly does change the taste of foods preserved in it, which is a good thing when we're used to the results, like pickled cukes, but might taste very odd with other food we might like to preserve, like potatoes. But some cultures pack just about everything in vinegar, and when you marry those people, they make you eat that stuff at Christmas time.

Obvious things to pack in vinegar

Nasturtium seed capers, mushrooms, many vegetables, garlic scapes (the green twisty tendrils that grow on the top of garlic stems) and some fruits.

▬ Garlic Scape or Dilly Bean Recipe ▬

Ingredients

2 pounds (1 kilogram) garlic scapes (can be
   replaced with green beans)
Canning salt
Water
Pickling vinegar
Honey
Balsamic vinegar
1 teaspoon cayenne pepper per jar (optional)
Several cloves garlic, divided
Pickling spice

Boil up a big pot of water to process your jars. Line your clean jars on the counter and gather together your ingredients. Pick the garlic scapes or beans at a young stage so they'll be tender. Wash them off under running water. You can cut the straight parts off the scapes and pack them upright in the jars, or you can twist the scape around in the jar horizontally until they are in tight rings. If you are using green beans, trim the ends off. The amount of liquid you will need will depend on how tightly you pack your jars, so pour some water in to a packed jar, and pour it back out into a measuring cup to find a liquid measurement you will need.

Figure your ratio of liquid as 1/3 water to 2/3 white vinegar. Count your jars and do your math, and put the water and vinegar on to boil. You can add either pepper flakes or curry powder to this hot liquid. Meanwhile back at your jars, add 1 teaspoon of honey to each half pint jar, and 1/2-teaspoon balsamic vinegar to each jar, plus a pinch of salt, 1 teaspoon pickling spice and perhaps some young garlic segments. Pour boiling vinegar and water mix over the top leaving 1/2-inch headspace. Poke inside each jar to remove air bubbles. Place two-part lids onto each jar, place them in your big canning pot and make sure they have at least one inch of water over them. Once that water has reached a boil again, process them. Ten minutes for the garlic scapes or 45 minutes for the beans. Let them sit for at least two weeks before eating if you can.

Technique #7 — Packing in Salt

Now, to me, this is an exciting technique. Simple, elegant, and with incredible results. Salt will be difficult to find unless you remembered to buy quantities of it before the stores all snapped shut from an earthquake. However, once in the home, it will keep for years until you want to use it. But if you need it, you'll need it fast. Here's a perfect example. A windstorm has knocked all the power out in the area and you have a bit of meat in your freezer you would hate to lose. By packing this meat in salt or brine, you can keep it for days or weeks longer without spoilage.

Brine technique

After choosing a waterproof container that is deep enough for your meat stores to sit inside of, make up a brine by adding coarse salt to hot water until it dissolves. When it floats a potato or an egg, it is strong enough to be used as a preserving brine for meat.

Salt packing technique

Put a layer of rock salt in the bottom of a waterproof container and lay your meat on top of this. Rub salt hard into the meat itself. Cover with a cloth and put in your coolest room.

— Salted Vegetable Stock

Ingredients
1 pound leeks
1 pound tomatoes
1 pound onions
¾ pound parsley and chervil, mixed
½ pound turnips
½ pound celery
1 pound salt

Grind all the above (or halve recipe) with a meat grinder or food processor into a large bowl. Let stand overnight. The next day, remix the contents by hand. Pack into jars and store in a cool place. Add to soups or for stock to be used for poaching fish. This should last in storage for a year or more.

Note: This recipe is taken from *Keeping Foods Fresh: Old World Techniques & Recipes* (1999) that is published by Chelsea Green.

Benefits to packing in salt

Salt is easy to find; it is inexpensive and easy to store. Salting and brining techniques need no fancy equipment.

Drawbacks

Meat tastes extremely salty and has to be soaked and boiled before it can be consumed, therefore losing nutrients. Too much salt is bad for you. Remember to drink lots of water after eating salty foods liked cured meats, and to be very careful if you have high blood pressure.

Technique #8 — Brining (lacto-fermentation in salt)

Although I had read about this food preservation technique in *Keeping Food Fresh: Old World Techniques & Recipes* and had been completely intrigued by such simple preservation methods, I didn't get deeply hooked until I had a young chef from Vancouver named Andrea Potter come up and teach a workshop on lacto-fermentation. I particularly liked the part where we stuffed washed cucumbers into a jar, poured in brine, poked in some garlic and dill, and knotted a cloth over the top. When I pulled the cloth off my own experiment a couple of weeks later, there were brilliant, crunchy pickles all ready to go, and I put a new lid on them and stuck them in the fridge. Lacto-fermentation occurs when lactic microbial organisms convert the natural sugars in the food into lactic acid. We know that an acid state prevents other critters from moving in. However, it also makes food more digestible and healthy. Our best known of lacto-fermented foods is sauerkraut, but many other veggies can be preserved this way too. I see this as a brilliant idea for extended power outages when we just have to save fridge or garden food for later.

Getting salt from the sea

It should be easy for West Coasters like me to get salt. The ocean is full of it. Our problem is finding unpolluted areas to gather seawater from. If we feel confident that the water is reasonably clean, we can gather some into a clean bucket, filter it through a cloth into a roasting pan on the woodstove or other constant heat source, and boil it down until it frees up its magical crystals of salt.

Ratios for making brine

2 tablespoons per quart OR 3 tablespoons per 1–1.5 liter OR for two liters (½ gallon) water, use ¼ cup and 1 tablespoon of salt. Dissolve in hot water.

Benefits to packing in brine

Salt is easy to find if you buy it beforehand, and is easy to store. It is inexpensive. Salting and brining techniques need no fancy equipment.

Drawbacks

Too much salt is bad for you. Some salted foods can be soaked, like meats, but you should always drink lots of water when eating salty foods.

Technique #9 — Packing in Oil

Sardines, stuffed vine leaves and sun dried tomatoes — many of our common oil packed foods have ancient beginnings. And naturally, the idea sprang, or even sprung, from a region of the planet where oil was plentiful — the Mediterranean. And what worked a couple thousand years ago is still good now. Oil will come in handy for saving the odd food type, though during an earthquake, it is not often that you hear the cry, "Oh my Gawd, save the olive oil so we can make stuffed vine leaves!" But cooking oil is on the Earthquake Kit list, and if you pour some over say, the half thawed cheese from a deceased freezer, you will still have the cheese, and you can still pour the oil off to cook with. Although many cooked veggies can be packed in oil to preserve them, remember to top the jar up with oil so no tip is exposed to the air when you put them away again.

Oil Packed Cheese

Chop cheese so that it can be packed into a clean jar. Pack as much cheese in as possible. Pour in oil until it is covered, screw on the lid and keep in a cool, dark place.

Veggies in oil

The rule of thumb for preserving oiled veggies seems to be that they are simmered in salted water or vinegar, then drained, packed into jars (with a sprinkling of salt or tablespoon of lemon juice) and covered with oil. Please consult the resource books at the end of this chapter, because it really is a simple process with delicious results.

Benefits to packing in oil

Food maintains a full taste, you need no extra oil to heat or cook the food. And in a pinch, you have the extra oil to pour off to use for other things.

Drawbacks

Oil is something we cannot make out of thin air. This means that we should be buying it ahead so there is always some on hand. Like all the other condiments, too much oil in the bloodstream is a bad thing. Remember to drain foods well before you eat them. Packing in oil assumes you have a steady supply — this worked in Ancient Greece, surrounded by olive trees, but is not so successful on the coast of British Columbia.

Technique #10 — Freezing

Freezing excess food seems an obvious choice, and one would wonder why it is tucked back at the last of the list, that is until the power goes out. We take the freezers that come with our refrigerators, and their bigger cousins in the back room, for granted until something goes wrong. A cord gets pulled out, a tree falls on a power line miles away, and pounds of precious food are turned to a sloppy mess. Some of us might shrug and phone the insurance company, but those on the lower end of the economic scale, living without insurance and who might have spent many hours assembling that little safety net, will have to absorb a crushing loss.

Losing my fridge freezer contents twice in one year smartened me up. Now I pressure can at least half the valuables, and keep the freezer for bread and pies and cheese, packed around only with what I figure I can afford to lose. But for most humans, freezing is the natural technique. Left over dinner can get scraped into a jar and tucked into the freezer for soup or another dinner. The heel of bread, half a pie and other treats get wrapped in plastic and in they go, safe and sound. To make sure freezers do their best for us, it is important to bag things well in thick layers of paper or plastic and seal them up tight to reduce spoilage.

Keep an indelible pen in your cutlery drawer as a reminder to label the contents as they go into the freezer. No more unrecognizable balls of tinfoil! Now at least you'll know what was in that tinfoil when you drag it out three years later. That's right, don't forget to date your freezer stash. And though thinking them anal at the time, I now have a secret respect for people who buy racks for their freezers so they can pull out bread, frozen veggies, or berries, without having a cascade of jars and bags collapse around them, like I do.

A word on blanching

Yes, I thought that blanching was the funny face people made when they heard bad news, but apparently there are broader meanings. Blanching is actually a pretty important part of the whole freezing process, since by using this step, you stop enzyme action in your food so that it preserves better in terms of taste, texture, appearance and nutritional values. An interesting fact:

Blanching, despite the hot water bath, keeps Vitamin C levels higher much longer than in unblanched foods.

Blanching concepts
Freshly picked and washed veggies are dropped into boiling water long enough (frequently only 2–3 minutes) to stop enzyme action, and then are transferred immediately to a cold water bath — either a bowl of ice water or a sink of very cold water. Once the food feels cool to the hand, pack it immediately into containers and place into the freezer.

Benefits of freezing
We can toss a loaf of bread, a slice of pizza, and half a bag of strawberries in there, and it will still be there in four years when we hack it out with a chisel. Many foods, with the exception of oily fish, keep well for months or a year if properly prepared and wrapped.

Drawbacks
Besides the one on your fridge, freezers are huge and one needs space to store them. If a freezer is not well managed, food gets misplaced and therefore wasted. Poorly wrapped foods dehydrate and lose nutrients. And if the power goes out, freezers aren't much good to us.

Obvious things to freeze
Just about anything can be thrown into a freezer, but if you're short on space, save it for low-acid foods that would do poorly being canned such as peas and beans and cooked meats, and it's a good place for your breads and buns.

Getting There from Here
1. **Stock up on pickling salt, sugar and honey, oil and canning jars.** You can practice now, or at least you will have supplies when you need them!
2. **Consider starting a supply co-op in your community,** with a food dehydrator, canning supplies and maybe a pressure canner or juicer or steamer.
3. **Think about how these items could be purchased and shared.**

The system we use in our community is that the person who keeps a particular piece of equipment at their house is responsible for it. You might try charging a deposit against the equipment, and/or a low daily charge. This will create respect for the equipment, and may build some repair money if things go wrong.

4. **Cruise the new or used book stores for food preservation books.** Things haven't changed much in the last few hundred years so it doesn't matter if the book is old. But do follow all instructions perfectly.

5. **Learn to dry a few items in your home.** You might try carrots and onions, and then go through the cycle of re-hydrating them and making soup.

Resources

Aubert, Claude, ed. *Keeping Food Fresh, Old World Techniques & Recipes*. White River Jct., Vermont: Chelsea Green Publishing, 1999.

   Another "must-have" food security book. Casual but tried and true preservation methods that also sound delicious.

Hupping Stoner, Carol, ed., *Stocking Up: How to Preserve the Foods You Grow, Naturally*. Emmaus, PA: Rodale Press, 1977.

   I have never felt I needed to update this old classic, and I still pull it out at least once a year. Thorough and methodical, this is a great way to learn the whys as well as the hows of food preservation of every kind.

Katz Ellix, Sandor. *Wild Fermentation: The Flavor, Nutrition, and Craft of Live-Culture Foods*. White River Junction, Vermont: Chelsea Green Publishing, 2003.

   This book illustrates how to make the most of natural fermentation to produce bread, yoghurt, cheese, beer, wine, sauerkraut, kimchi and other fermented foods.

CHAPTER 7

Just a Cup of Tea for Me or Hot Bevies from a Cool Garden

A chapter on tea drinking may sound absurd from a food security perspective, but peer deeply at the leaves in this particular teacup and we'll see where the mysterious values lie.

That deceptively transparent mixture of leaves and hot water has an ancient history that appears in many cultures, as an anchor for family, companionship, and the hour of the day. We can see it as a familiar comfort, a way of sharing repast, an approved method for welcoming almost any stranger, or merely as a way to warm up a chilled interior, but we are also receiving all the water-soluble health benefits that a plant has to offer us.

Below is a description of an interesting bunch of leaves we have available to us. This information was gleaned from the botanists and other scientists who share their studies at Plants for a Future, a resource center for useful plants, especially those containing edible and medicinal properties.

[This plant] can protect the teeth from decay, because of the fluoride naturally occurring.... The leaves are cardiotonic, diuretic, expectorant, stimulant and astringent. They exert a decided influence over the nervous system, giving a feeling of comfort and exhilaration, but also producing an unnatural wakefulness when taken in large doses. They are used internally in the treatment of diarrhea, dysentery, hepatitis and gastro-enteritis...is reportedly effective in clinical treatment of amoebic dysentery, bacterial dysentery, gastro-enteritis, and hepatitis. It has also been reported to have antiatherosclerotic effects and vitamin P activity. Excessive use, however, can lead to dizziness, constipation, indigestion, palpitations and insomnia.

Wow! Hot water can extract a lot of power from a handful of leaves. What is in that simple cup that we take so much for granted? It's an objective analysis of the *Camellia sinensis* — mother plant of both Chinese and English tea.

One of the earliest and yet most complete records of this particular plant used as tea was a Chinese scroll brushed between 760 and 780 AD. This scroll, "The Classic of Tea" by Lu Yu, not only refers to "a thousand and ten thousand teas" and the many cultivation and processing methods, he also records the legend that introduced this plant to fame in 2737 BC. In it, the Emperor Shen-Nung was boiling a pot of water when some young leaves from a nearby plant fell willy-nilly into it. He drank it anyway, was impressed as all get out, and history for this important plant proceeded from there. However, it's very likely that other cultures already used leaves in water as a food or beverage.

Here's a traditional middle Eastern plant/water blend. See if you can guess which commonly used drink this is:

[This plant has] traditionally been used in the treatment of fevers, headaches, digestive disorders (especially flatulence) and various minor ailments. The herb is abortifacient, anodyne, antiseptic, antispasmodic, carminative, cholagogue, diaphoretic, refrigerant, stomachic, tonic and vasodilator. An infusion is used in the treatment of irritable bowel syndrome, digestive problems, spastic colon etc. Externally a lotion is applied to the skin to relieve pain and reduce sensitivity... The essential oil in the leaves is antiseptic and strongly antibacterial...

Enough, already? Okay, that's peppermint tea, served frequently, often daily in many cultures. Note: The above paragraph is from "Peppermint," *Plants for a Future* database that is available online at pfaf.org.

It's likely that the earliest people noticed animals and birds thriving from drinking from leaf-filled pools and puddles. Ancient people were already familiar with hundreds of seeds, leaves, bark, roots and as soon as that first cooking pot was invented, were likely brewing up this warm, self-contained nutrient package.

Most of the benefits of a great number of plants are water soluble, so we can see how easily we can receive goodness from our surroundings with just a little knowledge.

Let's look at some terms, and then go out and do a little experimenting.

Filter: At the end of infusing your leaves in water, you'll want to separate the leaves back out so you can sip easily. You'll need something to strain the plant matter out of the water with. This could be a coffee filter with sticks pushed through it hung over a bowl or it could be a piece of clean cloth tied over the top of a jar, a tea ball or a clean sock. It depends where you are! When filtering, squeeze the filter at the end to force out the remaining goodness hiding within the plant matter.

Tea: Although formally, tea is any beverage made from a plant called *Camellia Sinensis*, which is dried, fermented, toasted and blended to bring us abundant tea varieties, many now call any hot plant-based beverage a tea, and my graphics shop guy, Charles, gives me heck for using those two terms interchangeably.

Tisane: Charles's way of describing a non-caffeinated hot herb beverage. And he's right!

Hot Infusion: Chop fresh or dried plant parts as finely as you can, place them in a container with a lid, pour just boiled water over this, stir or shake, put the lid on and let this sit for half an hour. Strain this off to drink and squeeze the remaining plant matter in a cloth. You can dilute the filtered infusion with more water if it's too strong. One reason not to boil your leaves or berries is because there may be Vitamin C in them (a valuable commodity) or other constituents affected by high heat that you don't want to diminish.

Cold infusion: I know you're smart, so you know this means doing the above, only with cold water, especially if that is all you have. But since hot water dissolves cell walls faster than cold water, cold infusions and decoctions generally sit for many hours, or overnight.

Decoction: Some plant parts take longer to release energy into the water. Roots and bark take longer for cell walls to dissolve than thin leaves. Soak these in cold water for a few hours, then gently raise the heat to a simmer, then keep it there for at least fifteen minutes in case there are some constituents that require heat before being released into your water.

Steep: This refers to the act of letting a tea sit. After adding the boiling water, or pouring the boiling water over the leaves, the pot should *steep* for at least a few minutes, lid on and heat off.

Cold cordial: Rinse berries (e.g., mountain ash berries, salmonberries, sumac cones, blackberries). Crush them into three times the volume of cold water, let it all sit for a couple of hours, filter and add honey to taste.

Hot cordial: Rinse berries (e.g., huckleberries, kinnikinnik, Oregon grape berries or rose hips, blackberries, salal berries or crab apples). Slice lengthwise and scrape out the seeds and any fine hairs as they can irritate the throat. Place in a pan, cover with water and bring to a simmer. Smash berries into the water, simmer, filter and add honey to taste. Chill for a cold cordial.

Coffee extenders: Some plant parts, particularly roots like dandelion and chicory, and the roasted seeds of broom, do make good coffee extenders. They make lousy coffee, though. But should you ever be in a position to look at your half pound of green beans and realize it will be difficult to plump up your supply in the near future, coffee extenders are your buddy! I have served these to my parents and friends with nary a raise of the eyebrows. These roots are at their sweetest in the spring. By fall, you may have to simmer your roots in water and change the water a couple of times before using, because they could be awfully bitter.

But if it does happen to be spring, here's the procedure: Go into your unsprayed back garden and carefully dig up any dandelion or chicory roots. Chop off the green top, scrub off any soil, and chop the roots into pencil eraser lengths. Bite into one, and if your mouth does a huge double take with the bitterness, steam or boil the roots for a few minutes, cool one off and try again. Some bitterness is good. Dry these slices in a warm, dry place such as a slow oven or over a woodstove. Grind them and blend them with your pathetically tiny supply of java juice, either by adding a tiny bit or all the way up to half the quantity by bulk. It ain't perfect, but sometimes it's really good.

Next time you walk out your door, try to identify plants that can be used as a tea. Naturally, taking plants from a very clean place is hugely preferable to taking them from a roadside, a parking lot or abandoned lot, but see what you can manage. Take a snip of that plant home with you and toss it into a cup of hot water, let it steep for at least five minutes, and then smell the aroma, and sip it. An experiment I do with my Little Sprouts class of avid seven-year-old botanists is to walk around the yard and take snips of lots of varied plant bits. After that we put them all in different bowls of hot water, let them sit, then sniff and taste them to decide which ones we like. The kids have decided that lawn grass and chives make bad tea while mints and sage make good tea. They have discovered their own good taste through experimentation.

In the Garden

Many veggie gardens have a few herbs in them. But if you haven't got them now, find some lemon balm, any of the mints, monarda, chicory flowers, red clover blossoms, pineapple weed or sage. And if you have wild strawberries within your reach, tossing one of the tiny fresh or dried berries into your tea will bring the most ambrosial scent to your brain.

In the Woods

Douglas fir, Western hemlock, fireweed leaves (make it strong or blend with stronger herbs), huckleberry leaves, dried kinnikinnik leaves, Labrador tea, dried nettle leaves, yarrow leaves and flowers, pine needles, spruce needles, currant leaves and berries, wild strawberry leaves and fruit, sumac, thimbleberry leaves and fruit, violet leaves and blackberry leaves can all be used in hot infusions. Begin tasting and experimenting to find the plants that bring you a feeling of health and pleasure. Oh, and did I remind you that this was all free?

Growing Herbs for Tea...er, Tisane

Organic herb teas are being rediscovered as a tonic boost, and can be simple to grow and are effortless to use. The top few inches clipped off a peppermint plant, dropped into a warm teapot and covered with hot water will release the most delightful scent. Mints are at their most maintenance free in one of the slightly damper, shadier parts of the yard. They grow happily in neglected corners such as beside the garden shed or at the foot of an old fence so they won't waste any precious space in your main garden.

Lemon balm and *Monarda* (also known as bergamot or bee balm) are two other tea plants that grow happily in part shade, and will require far less watering in this location. They can be treated like peppermint and dropped fresh into the teapot, but they also make a wonderful scented garnish for any summer food. Monarda flower petal's bright red hue also brighten a salad wonderfully and add a sweet and lightly pungent taste.

If you'd like to preserve your plants for winter teas, begin snipping branches off near the bottom third of its height in midsummer to hang upside down to dry. Harvest up to one third of the number of plant stems at one time, and allow it to recover before taking another third later on. If you don't take more than two cuttings, you'll get years out of a plant if you treat it right. Just make sure all cuttings are clean and dry, check carefully for bugs, and label each cluster of stems carefully. Hang all your herbs in a semi-dark, airy, warm place until the leaves can be crushed between your fingers. Then pop the leaves into a bag or jar.

Winter plant care is minimal, and can increase your yield for future seasons. Just rake fallen leaves over and around the plants, being sure to cover the root areas. That's all the fussing they should need, except for the odd summer watering if the chosen site is too sunny. If you find you are watering often, it means a move to a shadier site with some mulching is in order, so that you can spend more time in the hammock.

To establish a new tisane garden, wait for early fall so that the soil is cool and damp and the plants can adapt without stress. Once you've chosen a site, clear any existing garden or bush back and break the soil up. Place a layer of compost or mulch if the soil is especially poor. None of the above plants need a rich soil so no other soil preparation should be necessary. (Phew! I love my herb garden!) Make your shopping trip for young plants just after those first fall rains. Once home, untangle the roots of your young buddies, place them in their new site and soak them well. Mulch the area to keep the soil moist and cool. That space between summer's intense heat and the first frost offers a stress-free time for your plants to settle in and establish sound roots (with a bit of water if those rains are late), and they will start up again in the spring with great energy and little help. If you really feel like meddling, just pull away the leaf mulch to let the spring sun boost new growth. These plants will have a head start over anything you could plant in late spring, and will need less watering because they will already have a well-established root system.

Just about all of the above named plants can be dried for future use. Here are some basic suggestions for drying plant matter for teas:

- Choose healthy looking plants from a clean area.
- Pick plant and leaf matter on a dry day, when the dew is off but before blazing sunlight hits them, if possible.
- Dry leaves as quickly as possible, one layer deep on rack, or by hanging in an airy but shaded room.
- When they are crunchy to the touch, pull the leaves off the stems and pack into paper bags or jars.
- Store these in a dry place. Don't powder the leaves or break them too small at this point, as you can lose volatile oils by crushing the cells open.
- Wait until just before making the teas to break them up small.

Field Study (literally!!)

1. On your next walk in your community, identify five wild plants that can be used as a tea.
2. If you don't have any herbs in your garden, find someone who will share garden herbs for you to try as a hot drink.
3. Practice drying three types of plant that can be used later for a hot beverage.
4. Buy some honey to make this experience even better.

Resources

Website

Plants for a Future: Edible, Medicinal and Useful Plants for a Healthier World, pfaf.org.

This UK charity is compiling a database, which currently houses approximately 7000 species of plants. The database contains not only edible and medicinal uses, but lists plants used for dyes, adhesives, inks and fibers.

Books

Antol, Marie Nadine. *Healing Teas, How to Prepare and use Teas to Maximize your Health*. New York: Avery Publishing Group, 1995.

This book provides many details on the history and use of green teas, and plenty of information on many other herbs, including medicinal uses.

Stewart, Hilary. *Wild Teas and Cordials: 60 Drinks of the Pacific Northwest.* Vancouver: Douglas and McIntyre Ltd., 1981.

A sweet, straightforward book with line drawings for identification and simple recipes for culinary drinks. Could be either great fun, or superb in an emergency.

CHAPTER 8

Please Don't Eat the Daisies (Without a Good Dressing)

Why would a food security handbook have a chapter on flowers? First...the Big Picture!

The Food, It Was Just Hiding There

Like most people visiting Asia, I have experienced the constant dripping of a rain of epiphanies during my stays. One of these occurred on a trip to Northern Thailand, as I was standing at the edge of a new friend's yard. I admired the grove of towering bamboo that edged her garden boundary, in a row so straight I could have marked it off with a piece of thread, with not a single trace of bamboo growing out into the road.

"How do you do that?" I asked her. "How do you keep the bamboo from growing all over the place, outside of your yard?"

"Well, that's easy," she replied. "Everyone knows how good bamboo shoots are in their dinner. The minute one shows its head outside of my garden, someone takes it home."

"Oh," I said, "In Canada, we hack down the bamboo and throw it in bushes, and buy bamboo shoots in a can at the store".

But that is what North American culture is all about. We have been trained that if it is right in front of our face (e.g., free, accessible) it is somehow inferior, and that the only really good stuff is at the store. The more abundantly and freely something grows, the more reviled it should be. Bamboo is just one example. I wonder if people would treat it with more respect if they knew that they could learn to peel and boil those shoots. Bamboo would no longer seem invasive; it would become a treat. And kudzu, long hated in the Southern U.S. is another good example. Years ago, this plant was established by the new Asian population as a survival plant. The starchy roots and shoots grow easily and are very digestible, the young leaves, flowers and unripe pods are edible cooked or raw, and older leaves are used in tea. This is also a fodder plant, so farm animals could glean a meal as well. And the Asians also knew that kudzu was an ancient Chinese medicine (ge gen) used extensively for many conditions, including alcoholism. But it's just another noxious weed now, since no one keeps it at bay by eating the healthful roots and shoots, and people can't get rid of it fast enough to drink their beer and eat their not so easily digested Twinkies in peace.

North Americans are also famous for ripping out so-called weeds such as huckleberry and salal, plants that are perfectly adapted to our climate, so that they have a place to put nice pots of petunias. But you can't eat petunias. And we all know about the infamous scourge, the Himalayan blackberry. A friend pointed out that if there was something worth smoking in blackberry roots, there wouldn't be a plant left standing in three weeks. But while he's out there, puffing tentatively away in the back yard, we can eat, freeze, and make wine out of the tons of berries that come off these plants each year.

Additionally, peppermint and lemon balm always come with a warning to keep them contained or they will run amok, which is just proof that someone isn't drinking enough locally picked herb tea.

And what to do with those orange day lilies, the ones considered *common*, that seem to need thinning and composting each year? It might be time to just eat them! I can't wait for the flowers to begin folding up in the evening, so I can chop them into a salad (although I hear they're nice fried, too), and this year I might have enough plants to try eating the young shoots. Calendula is great in salad too, and the clovers make great tea. At any rate, now that we know about that overabundance problem we have in our yards, let's tackle it a bit at a time by chowing down on our edible flowers.

An Extremely Compressed List of Edible Flowers

Most of these are a pleasure to eat raw and some need to be blended in a salad.

Basil: Flowers good in tomato dishes.

Begonia: Dessert or garnish.

Borage: Candied, frozen into ice cubes for summer drinks.

Calendula: Edible and medicinal, used to dye eggs and rice, scattered into salad.

Carnation/Dianthus: Herb butters and salads. Remove white heel as it's bitter.

Chives: Salads, oil and vinegar, anywhere you need an onion bite.

Chrysanthemum: Fried.

Clover: Good in tea or salad. Kids love sucking the nectar out of them.

Daylily/Tiger lily: Chop into salads, fry or pickle.

Dill: Salads, eggs, potatoes.

Elder: Tempura, tea.

Geranium: Scented waters for jams and vinegars.

Hibiscus: Stuff with mango bits, eat fresh in salads.

Hollyhock: Salads.

Honeysuckle: Frittered.

Lavender: Vinegars, tonic waters.

Lemon Verbena: Teas, to flavor jellies, ice cream, garnish.

Mallow: Salad.

Marigold: See calendula.

Meadowsweet: Beautiful scent.

Mint: Teas, desserts, bathwater.

Nasturtium: Salad and sandwiches.

Primula/Primrose: Right off the plant, mild sedative.

Rose: Syrups and waters, pickle the rosebud, cook into fruit pies (remove white heel).

Rosemary: Infusion for the face, put in salads, Italian dishes.

Sage: Salads and teas.

Squash: Stuff with food mixtures, made into soup.

Viola/Pansy family: Good garnish, salads, ice cubes and fruit desserts.

Yucca: Remove bitter middle part. Eat raw or cooked in salads or stir-fry.

When we start looking at the options, we realize there are probably a few good meals' worth of flowers in our gardens if we just started to use them as food. Some plants create an abundance all at once (like the elderberry blossoms) and some produce over a long period of time (squash blossoms). Some fill out a meal, and some are tiny offerings that will not amount to much bulk, like the dainty violet, but are a pleasure to the senses.

Well, we're hot on this now. But how do we eat the darn things? My favourite method is to just snap them off the plant and eat them in the garden as a little snack. One of the pleasures of my "walk-and-talk" classes is to gently pick a lily flower, peel off and eat one of the big, rich petals, and to then hand the remaining flower to the student behind me. There is usually a cautious bite, then a surprised smile, and the flower gets passed down the line with little smiles popping up as the blossom disappears down the row. Lilies produce lots of flowers and they do possess bulk. A large handful will take the edge off an appetite. None of mine make it into the house for cooking but I am waiting anxiously for next year, because this time I really am going to hold off and get them all the way into the house and cook them before I eat them. Really!

Many other flowers do make it inside and I chop them into multi green salads. Chive and fennel flowers, bergamot and calendula are my favourite, but any would do, especially herb flowers. I add my usual salad dressing, a simple mix of oil, lemon juice, garlic and a spoonful of mayo, and it dresses up any combo of greens and flowers. And hoping they aren't wasted, I use lots for garnish on my famous Robin's devilled eggs, potato or pasta salads or just about any dessert.

I like having lots of squash in the garden for winter food, and since squash are famously giddy for mixing up their male/female dating equation, there are always lots of wallflowers left over for me to bring in for a hot dinner. I check for any lazy bees, pinch off the innocent and possibly virginal bystander, peel off the thick green calyx around the base and lay those kids in a row on the counter. There are exotic recipes as shown below, but I simply pop a little square of cheese into each orange throat, twist it shut, then toss the cheese filled flowers into a paper bag filled with flour, salt and pepper. This is then dumped into a hot frying pan with some olive oil and garlic in it, covered, cooked for just five minutes with one turn of the spatula, and then slid onto the edge of any summer meal.

Lilies can be served the same way, and either of them, along with other big strong flowers like elderberry clusters, can be dipped in batter and fried, like a tempura. Stuff the lilies with ricotta, or add them to an omelette. Health nuts can just steam them, or chop them into soups. Both lilies and squash can be eaten at any stage from tight bud to drooping oldster. (Note: Don't say the words "drooping" and "oldster" in front of certain oldsters.) I like to leave flowers for the bees to feed on before I harvest them. You can dry lily flowers and reconstitute them later for use, and next year I'm going to try pickling them.

Here is a recipe from the book *Edible Wild Plants of Eastern North America* by Merritt Lyndon Fernald and Alfred Charles Kinsey.

These fellows suggest nipping off the fat buds or newly opened flowers of the lily and dipping them in a batter of beaten egg, milk, flour and seasoning, and then frying them in oil or butter. This is a quick meal with only a five-minute cooking time and a couple of flippings.

That sounds scrumptious. And then we have...

▬ Squash Flower Soup ▬

Ingredients
1 to 2 tablespoons butter
1 chopped up onion
1 or 2 cloves garlic, minced
2–4 cups chicken broth or vegetable stock
Squash blossoms equal to the number of cups of broth
½ cup milk or cream
1 cup half and half
Salt and freshly ground pepper to taste
Top with available cheese.

Melt the butter in a good-sized saucepan. Sauté the onions and garlic with the salt and pepper. Cook until onions are soft. Add the broth or veggie stock and bring to a boil, then simmer. Add the blossoms and let them cook down for several minutes. Toss this into the blender or food processor for a bit of a mash, then put it back into the pan and add the milk and then top with cheese if you like, clogged arteries permitting.

Squash Blossom Frittata

Ingredients
Several squash blossoms
1-2 baby squash
4 eggs
Splash of milk
2 green onions
Asiago cheese
Chopped parsley and snipped chives (optional)
Salt and pepper to taste

Pick 3 to 4 blossoms per person and a couple of immature squash, if you have them. (You can check for immaturity by asking them the Ancient Cucurbita riddle. *If the squash gods are all-powerful, can they make a squash so big that they themselves cannot lift it?* A truly immature squash will, frankly, be flummoxed by this question.) Beat the eggs with a little milk. Add fresh chopped parsley and chive flowers, if desired. Add salt and pepper to taste.

In your frying pan, sauté a little butter and cook the green onion and thinly sliced baby squash just until soft. Then quickly sauté the blossoms for about 30 seconds and remove from pan.

Pour the egg mixture into the pan, place the onions, squash and blossoms on top and cook over low to medium heat until almost set. Sprinkle with asiago cheese and put under the broiler until lightly puffed and browned.

This recipe was adapted from the Seasonal Chef website listed at the end of this chapter.

Pasta With Day Lily Buds and Mushrooms

Ingredients
About 6 oz. of oyster or shiitake mushrooms
1 heaping cup daylily buds, 1½ to 2 inches long
2 tablespoons unsalted butter
2 tablespoons olive oil

2 shallots, finely minced

½ teaspoon freshly chopped marjoram

1 tablespoon fresh chopped parsley

Salt and pepper to taste

Freshly grated parmesan cheese

1 pound. fresh fettuccine noodles

Put water on to boil while preparing vegetables. Clean mushrooms, do not rinse. Use either brush or damp paper towel. Tear into large bite size pieces and remove stem of shiitakes. Rinse the daylily buds and pat dry. In large skillet, heat butter and oil over medium heat. Add the shallots and sauté them for a couple of minutes. Add mushrooms and stir for 1 or 2 minutes. Add the daylily buds and stir for 2 to 3 minutes. Add the herbs and season to taste with salt and pepper. Cover the skillet and let stand over low heat for a few minutes while pasta is cooking. Drain the pasta, add it to the vegetables, and toss well. Add another tablespoon of butter or oil if necessary. Taste for seasoning and serve hot. Garnish with breadcrumbs and parmesan if desired.

Note: This recipe is taken from the website Outdoor Elements, wnit.org/outdoorelements/ (February 26, 2008).

▬ Pickled Lily Buds ▬▬▬▬▬▬▬▬▬▬▬▬

Pick 2 quarts (8 cups) closed lily buds, pinch off the stems, dust off any garden refuse and steam these for up to 20 minutes, then drain. Pack these artfully into half pint jars. Or just cram them in there. Time's a wastin'.

Meanwhile, in another saucepan blend 3 cups vinegar, ¾ cup packed brown sugar, salt, allspice, nutmeg and cloves to taste. Bring to a boil for a few minutes. Pour vinegar mixture over the packed buds. Quickly apply the 2 part sealing lids. Yield: 8 half-pints (250 ml size). Pack away for a few weeks before eating so that the spices can settle into the buds.

Drying Flowers for Winter

If you'd like to save flowers for later meals, you can always dry them. Elder blossoms, calendula, clover and chamomile, and mint and other herb flowers dry easily on bamboo mats or racks. I harvest them like I do my herb greens, picking them when the dew is off. Make sure to dust off any chunky bits, check well for bugs, and place the flowers a single layer deep in shallow baskets, putting them up high in a shady, airy room. During the height of summer they dry within days, and then they go into paper bags. People in drier climates could put them in a jar, but I worry about the humidity in moist climates like where I live on the West Coast, and the blossoms stay vibrant in the paper bags, so I have stopped worrying. Next year I will try drying the bigger flowers like lily and squash blossoms.

Goals

1. Learn to identify five edible flowers.
2. Make one new recipe that will incorporate flower blossoms into a meal.

Resources

Website

Seasonal Chef. seasonalchef.com/recipe0805b.htm (accessed Febuary 23, 2008).

This website brings together chefs who wish to cook using local ingredients and links them up with local producers. It lists many recipes and offers resources from cookbooks to citrus juicers.

Books

Couplan, François. *The Encyclopedia of Edible Plants of North America: Nature's Green Feast*. Chicago Illinois: McGraw-Hill Publishing, 1998.

I could have placed this resource book into almost any chapter, but in this case, the notes for plants mentions whether the flower is eaten, and sometimes how.

Leggatt, Jenny. *Cooking With Flowers*. London: Century, 1987.

Sorry about the age of this book, folks! It's the only one I have, and I found it at a used book store. It suggests lots of ways of working flowers of all kinds into your daily meals, and has recipes for petal jams, crystallized flowers and other painstaking delights I will try when I am rolling in spare time.

CHAPTER 9

Gardener
With a Suitcase

Now that we have decided that one of the many benefits of gardening (besides the fabulous pecs) is a greater sense of food security, what do we suggest to all those people who would love to grow some food but who forgot to have a million dollars to buy property with? Many of us, short or long term, end up in apartments or basement suites and have only small balconies or a strip along the sidewalk to call our own. And even if we rent a house, we may not want to "waste" our time putting in a veggie garden for what might be the next tenant.

For those of us with green thumbs, these issues can be very frustrating. And the first thing we have to remember is that although no situation is perfect, awkward circumstances are the best learning tools. Below are just a few ways to get our hands dirty, whether you're a land baroness or not.

- Garden at someone else's place (e.g., down the street, a friend's or at a community garden).
- Garden with what you have (e.g., container or balcony garden, lateral gardens, intensive gardening with tightly packed plants).
- Garden really fast (e.g., high nutrient greens, early varieties).
- If you are renting a house, put a garden in anyways and pretend you have forever. You might. Or begin the Perpetual Renters Garden as described in my essay *If I were Queen of the World* further along in this chapter.

Compromise #1 – Garden Somewhere Else

There is a consciousness re-forming that shared garden space is a good thing, so we are not starting from scratch here. Some small towns have community gardens, and you might find these by asking at a community services office or health unit. The local gardening clubs may already have a list of people seeking or wanting to share gardens. My own thought is that if your town lacks all of the above, then start your own with a poster or ad campaign.

Community gardens will generally come with their own set of rules, such as time of use, tool borrowing, watering times and cleanup, but when you share a private garden somewhere, you will have to create your own rules as you go along. It seems to be that new people sharing their private garden space with strangers are very prickly at first, but this dies down as they find a new presence in their garden is not a big threat to their privacy, and could be quite useful. Here are some tips for approaching the steward of a possible garden space.

- Offer to come during prearranged times, so that the homeowner finds it predictable and manageable. Alert them ahead of time if you have to change those hours.
- Be polite. Park your car out of the way, close gates, be kind to the dog, put hoses away and don't leave piles of soil on the lawn.
- Give back. A little basket or bag of young veggies on the doorknob is always a good gift.
- Be helpful. Offer a hand where you see it is needed. If there are problems with the garden, offer suggestions as to how you can help solve them rather than complaining about them.

And to the property owner sharing land, I would suggest you:
- Make your needs really clear from the start so there are no misunderstandings.
- Show the gardener where the tools are kept.
- Discuss hours that work for you. (Seeing a strange shape in the garden always scares the dickens out of me, until I remember a gardener was to come that day.)

It occurred to me, when I began to share garden space on my land, that I could charge a bit of rent on each garden bed and turn that into seed money. But I scrapped that idea and just mentioned that if there are ever too many veggies coming in at once, I would be happy to have some. Here is what I actually got, from my main garden user, Harry:

> One apple tree, planted and pruned; three garden beds hugely improved in tilth; all the late squash that he doesn't feel like picking; access of his purple kale and sprouting broccoli; a few seeds from his shallots; leeks and yellow peas; buckets of plants from his other garden; and garden advice and plant identification. And spring seedlings. And free hoses. I think the value is higher when letting others choose their own level of payment, whatever that may be, than ever charging cash for garden space, but you be the judge.

Speaking of garden advice, this can be the true bonus for the new gardener who is sharing an established patch at someone else's house. You'll get to see how the pros do it. Watch when and how things get planted and you'll find out all the local wisdom without having to learn it the hard way.

Compromise #2 – Garden With What You Have

Apartment living drives true gardeners wacky. Sometimes there is a little garden space about two feet wide on each side of a path, and sometimes a small cement space is available, either a landing or balcony. The eager gardener can go ahead and look for a shared planting area, however, he or she can also get big-time into container gardening.

I don't restrict container gardening advice to just apartment dwellers. Although I rented houses with perfectly good gardens for years, I traveled with the same pots of little trees and flowers for over a decade, and there is no harm in it. It is even a delight, upon moving to a new spot, to set your green kids out around the deck and doorway in all their familiar glory. You can arrange and rearrange with the season, moving sensitive plants into part shade if need be, which you can't do in a planted garden. Flowering and food items can come to the fore, then be gently shoved back when their prime time is over. And just think, when you

How to Feed your Containers and Tiny Gardens

Nope, you just can't ladle a forkful of horse manure onto that little lettuce you're growing. You'll have to mash it up small. One way to get large things into tiny pots or growing spaces is to make the famous "pòo tea," which does not actually have to contain manure, but...okay, it does stink! Find a large bucket or half barrel. If you have a comfrey plant available, shred some leaves into the bucket. Add some chickweed or other weeds and leaves, kitchen bits and manure if you have it, old drips from the teapot, coffee grounds and seaweed. Fill with water, and cut a nice tight fitting wooden lid for this bucket, with an old gate handle screwed on. Leave this to cook for a couple of weeks, then take a peek. It should be a seething mass of rotting vegetation, with a stink hard to describe to the layperson and the appearance of brown slime. Ah, a gardener's dream come true! Give this a good witch's stir, dip in a smaller bucket and scoop some out, dilute this down to a shade of weak tea, and water your containers or plants with this. Feed them often with this tea. Refill the barrel with water, refit that nice lid that you now love, and let it cook away some more.

finally settle, you will already have a lot of healthy plants to dig into your new garden.

If you want an idea of what would do well in a container, just visit a nursery and see what they have growing there. They may even have samples of mixed containers so you can get ideas for salad pots or herb combinations.

Tips for container growing

1. Choose the biggest containers you can find. They hold water better than little ones and have more root room.
2. Place them so you can water them easily. Most containers need daily watering in high summer.
3. Watch for weight if you are on a balcony. Place large containers near walls.
4. Don't assume containers need full sun. Most plants are happier with some cool or dappled shade for part of the day, because they cannot drive roots down to a cool place when they need rehydrating.
5. Remember to use lateral space, like a tiny trellis or pole in your pot to extend growing space, or have a tall plant with surrounding short ones.

Maybe you have more than a balcony or maybe there is a tiny yard available. In his book *The Edible Container Garden: Growing Fresh Food in Small Spaces* Michael Guerra says that 55 pounds (or 25 kilograms) of food from a parking space size garden is a possible goal. This would be pretty fancy footwork, mind you. You would have to train peach trees and grape vines up any available walls, train squash vines over a net, under which your greens and berries were growing, and this would take more than one season to get right. But all of these plants are pretty tough, even the peach tree will tolerate a fair amount of peach leaf curl and still produce well. And you would have to mulch like crazy to keep the soil rich and the micro-organisms busy and happy, but this is not difficult to master. Don't be afraid to crowd plants when you first place them. Perennials can be moved, and for several years before moving them, you will have a dense wall of currants, strawberries, cicely, peppermint and raspberries growing out of quite a tiny strip of soil. You can thin the smaller plants later and start new patches.

Some thoughtful tips for small space gardening are:

1. Using lateral space well, by creating structures like trellises and arches to train plants onto. Create plant hanging baskets with salad plants and a cherry tomato; attach plastic pots to a wall.

2. Crowding plants to maximize harvest, and feeding the soil well to support this.

3. Inter-planting, like tucking salad plants between growing garlic bulbs.

4. Succession planting, where more seedlings are ready to go in the minute old plants come out. An example would be placing tomatoes in after the purple sprouting broccoli has done its bit.

5. Select small varieties. For instance, a shallot is a wonderful thing chopped into a sandwich and can be stuck into a small space, bush beans take up little space but can give a treat in late summer. Veggies seed also comes in mini-size. There are half-long carrots and tiny cabbages or just pick things young such as baby beets.

Compromise #3 – Garden Really Fast

I used to wonder, when I flipped through my seed catalogues, why it mattered whether a carrot reached harvestable size in sixty-two or seventy-five days. I figured that people who counted stuff like that on the calendar really needed lives. But then my smart friend Maria reminded me that if she planted early potatoes (potatoes whose tops are dying down early, showing that the tubers below are ready to eat before other varieties) she would have her harvest in before the drought hit. And then I realized that those silly numbers besides the veggie photos could come in handy for other reasons, like the Gardener with a Suitcase. We can buy starts (and now I know why they call them starts as it gives you a head start on the season) in little flats from the nursery, and use our seed catalogues to pick the fastest veggies we can find.

And remember that even if you are living in a space for only three or four months, there's a lot that can be grown in that time. Take a walk through a good seed catalogue and make note of the time to maturity if you think your time is short in a garden. The following veggies, planted at the right time and given the right conditions, will grow damned fast. You'll be tempted to call in the Olympic drug squad on a few of these fellas.

Asian greens: 21–70 days
Bush beans: ready between 52–60 days
Carrots: 54–90 days.
Cauliflower: 50–90 days.
Chard: 50–60 days
Cucumbers: 56–62 days
Kale: 50–65 days
Lettuce: 35–70 days
Peppers: 58–80 days
Radishes: 25–60 days
Spinach: 45–50 days
Summer Squash: 40–60 days
Tomatoes: 65–90 days.

Compromise #4:
Make Transient Gardening the Trend it Should Be

When I moved to the Sunshine Coast from North Vancouver, I left a veggie garden behind, and it bugged me. But my new garden had a veggie patch already established, and as the man who had planted it pointed out all the ripe peppers I was going to fall heir to, I realized what a great chain this actually was. What if there was a garden, for every season, going on everywhere we moved to? Sure, there would be variations depending on our individual tastes, but what if leaving a garden only meant stepping into a new one? Sloppy or anal, big or small, the previous steward's mark would be printed loud on the living landscape, and we would slip into their place, changing the curtains, painting the bathroom and taking over another little patch of food.

If I Were Queen of the World

Okay, if I were Queen of the World, there would be some major international shakedowns, as expected. But I also would impose one tiny ruling that would surprise the renters and drifters of the world (who sometimes do have a reason to feel put upon already), and that would be that in every space they found themselves, they had to plant a food garden. "What?" I hear it now. "Why pick on us? We might have to move again. We can't afford to live anywhere for a long time. Life is already complicated. It wouldn't be worth it. It would be a waste of time."

Of course, since I was Queen, I would have all my arguments worked out. Home owners can at least feel that they have a relative amount of control over some of the things that happen within their fence boundaries. Renters often imagine they have nowhere in the world that they have a say over what goes on. They imagine that since they have no land to steward over, they have no power over the environment. They have no place where they can decide that bees should have flowers, that birds should have a clean place to nest, that one tiny truck can be removed from the fossil fuel chain by a herb tea patch. But I think that people should consider that the patch outside their door, no matter how small or trampled upon, is the only place they have true stewardship over, where they can offer peace and health to the planet, and they should take wild advantage of it. It doesn't matter if it's one meter wide and under a layer of beer cans.

So we should just go ahead and stick in flowers and tea plants, poke an overgrown potato under the soil, stick in some strawberries and some lettuce. We could learn to observe carefully, and that way we could get more in touch with the seasons and how they affect the bees and flowers. And while we're down there, we should say "hi" to a bug by helping it to hide with mulch and sticks, so it can have a safe life. Imagine if we started a movement where we made safe homes for other beings. Even small ones. Especially small ones. Bugs and bees are important, too. And drifters should not resent the effort they give to this, because it gives them power that they only think is becoming lost to them. And then when they move, there will one day be another garden by some other back door, already waiting for them, with fresh tea, and a few berries, and some humming bees. So right after the many other tasks I would set for myself, I would impose this gardening duty onto renters and other drifters as one of those things that would come back at us one day like a great big kiss. If I were Queen, that is.

Things To Do

1. Study the plants at a local nursery to see how well each plant seems to manage in a container. Some, like rhubarb and cosmos, just don't seem to like the small space, while others look perfectly content. Get a feel for what looks happiest.
2. Learn to admire balcony ideas, and look at them carefully for ideas.
3. Pick up a seed catalogue and look at the ranges of growing periods and vegetable sizes.
4. Begin looking at wooden boxes, old sinks and empty paint cans with a new eye — and begin collecting them for plant containers for your new mobile garden. Don't forget to drill holes in the bottoms of watertight containers.

Resources

Gazeley, Victoria. *Gardening on the Edge: The Busy Person's Beginner Guide to Growing Gourmet Vegetables on Your Patio, Balcony or Deck*. North Vancouver. Self-published, 2008.

Economical, practical and best of all, "do-able" organic food growing projects, tips and step-by-step advice for new urban gardeners.

Guerra, Michael. *The Edible Container Garden: Growing Fresh Food in Small Spaces*. New York: Fireside/Gaia Books, 2000.

This book gives gardeners with limited space practical tips on growing vegetables, edible flowers, fruits, and herbs in containers, window boxes, raised beds, trellises and more.

CHAPTER 10

Into the Wild

Many of us now understand that large groups of people lived in what is now called British Columbia, for many thousands of years, without benefit of supermarkets, refrigerated trucks, and especially peanut butter chocolate "Zig Zag" soya product frozen dessert. From all accounts, these were organized cultures, strong and healthy enough to create war as well as intricate art forms. Although the household nut that loves fishing will say, "Oh goody, this is the part where we go fishing" (right to assume that the First Nations people on the West Coast loved a good hunk of salmon as well as the next guy), they also relied on lots of alternative forest products for a full menu. Yes, you're right, I'm gently leading you outside to have a look at what grows pretty fiercely all over the ground. A lot of it is food. The First Nations folks had a few centuries to get into a pattern of harvest and storage, and it was hard work to glean as much as they could to survive a winter, but there is no harm in us knowing the basics. We might need to know some of this one day, and many of us live near, if not on, the forest edge, which is the prime area for most of the goodies the West Coast provides.

"Goodies?" you ask. "You're going to talk about roots and berries here, aren't you?" Yes, roots and berries, and stems and leaves. These plant products helped keep the whole omnivore population alive (even before omnivores used that many syllables) about a million years ago. Humans loved, dreamt, created philosophy and mathematics, all without the benefit of a local fast food establishment. The interesting part is, when anthropologists study ancient and existing medicines, they have to admit that cultures seemed to thrive without things like heart disease, hemorrhoids and Type II diabetes until the advent of, you guessed it, supermarkets and refrigerated trucks. Okay, there's no time for that right now, and ancient folk still did have their share of problems (like being cold and wet), but let's just say that humans ate from the planet's abundance for a long, long time, and it won't hurt to know how to supplement your diet from it if need be. You might even start to like it. And just think. No hemorrhoids or acne!

Opening the Front Door

This is an important first step in learning about wild foods. You actually have to go out there. And, like learning about computer components, it's best to have someone along at first who knows their stuff and can get you identifying the basics. And it's good to start off with a guide book, a paper bag, and a nice day, since you want your early experience to be positive. And a thermos of coffee and a good hat, but that's all. And a notebook. And maybe a pen. Okay, you can take some lunch and your camera. And that's all. And the car cushion. Yup, okay, and spare socks. And a chocolate bar, *and that's all.* Now stop fussing and just go outside!

If you are not already a plantie (there are foodies, so why can't there be planties?) learning how to identify local flora is a skill you can pick up quickly and with pleasure. The main component of plant identification is by familiarization through your senses, so that your brain, which is actually not just daydreaming about eating mangoes in Bali, can incorporate all that sensory input for careful long-term storage. So your helpful assistant is going to lead you over to a hemlock tree, or maybe you know this one yourself. You are going to thank the plant very much for opening your mind to its identity, then you will take a snippet off the end of a branch. Grind this between your fingers and give a good sniff. How long are the needles? How many come out of each pore, and how are they arranged on the stem? Give this a chew, lick your teeth, and then sniff your plant sample again. Put this sample in your bag and carry on. Go visit a cedar tree, and a pine, and repeat the process. Have your guide show you a thimbleberry bush. Give your usual thanks, then snip off the end of a branch. Let's widen your questioning now. Is the stem hollow or solid? Does sap run out? What does it smell like? Is the stem round or square? These are the types of questions you will take to each plant. The scents will begin to stick in your brain after a few visits, the feel and personality of each plant will become clear. Don't be afraid to taste as you go. Although many are afraid of biting into a poisonous plant, this method is a completely safe way to do this since it would be impossible, with even a very toxic plant, to get enough into your body to injure you using the bite-and-lick-your-teeth technique.

When you get home, empty your bag onto the table and line up your stems and leaves. How many do you remember? If you have kids, you will remember even better, because children are wild about this kind of thing. It will help your memory to tape a stem or leaf onto a piece of paper and label it, because the action of doing this will improve your recognition skills.

Roots and Shoots

Just like in a vegetable garden, the seasons have a strong influence over what will be available to you to eat outside. Obviously, roots are pretty dependable, because a plant has them all year round, and the native population cooked and ate sword fern roots, thistle and clover roots, and lots of lily tubers that are getting rare so I am not even going to mention them. Cinquefoil roots were dug in winter or spring, scraped, steamed and eaten and said to be quite like a sweet potato, and when my patch gets big enough, I will put that to the test. The whole dock family (most commonly the curled and western dock) has edible roots and shoots, and these may need to be boiled to soften, though the stem is likely to be more edible.

Even in my talks about eating strange wild foods, the first comment from an audience is usually "aren't you afraid of poisoning yourself?" Well, frankly, no. There are really not that many poisonous plants out there, and despite that, everything I choose to eat is easily recognizable, not visually similar to a toxic plant, and eaten in small enough amounts that it would not kill me at any rate. But it is a good idea with any new food to eat just a small amount and wait a few hours to see how your body likes it. Then if you feel fine after eating it, you can try a bit more.

Shoots, on the other hand, are generally best in spring, when they are just shooting up. The easiest to recognize and find and most common of the edible shoots are the salmon berry and thimbleberry. Cut these off, peel off the stem bark, and steam and eat. The young thimbleberry tips are good raw on a walk. These are still edible steamed later in the season, but as the plant matures into summer, they get awfully tough.

Another plant with a decent edible stem is the thistle. These plants are pretty easy to recognize (just wave your hand around one for a minute and that should just about do for permanent recognition) and any thistle you can find around here can be called food. You'll need some good gloves for this, but give it a try. Head over to your nearest thistle patch (mine was conveniently located on top of a desirable planting area) and use both hands to pull the stem, including the root, out of the soil. Snip the stem into lengths and peel the bark off. This can now be eaten raw, if it's young, or cooked. The root needs cooking and is apparently more of a survival food than the stem, but the nice thing is that no matter how long you pull out thistle stems, they will keep coming up in your garden. Good news, eh? And the leaves are actually edible but need those nasty prickles snipped off, and I have not taken the afternoon off yet to sit in the rain and do this, so can't swear by it as a substitute for, say, a walk on the beach to the fish and chips shack. But if I was really hungry, I could snip the prickles off the flower, and eat that, too.

Fireweed is another plant that is pretty recognizable and easy to find. This is another plant with an edible stem. Pick them young, and peel and steam or boil. The flowers are good in tea, but could also be added to dinner in a pinch.

The First Nations on the West Coast of Canada made good use of the native springbank clover, but all clovers can be harvested and used, like many plants, for more than roots and stems. The species we are most likely to trip over (and rip out) in our gardens is the red clover (*Trifolium pratense*) and let me bend your ear a moment about this particular plant. First, it fixes nitrogen so is a great soil improver. Second, all parts are edible and even nutritious. The young greens can be eaten raw in salads or cooked into meals. The flowering tops, fresh or dried, are not only tasty, but are gathering a long and very appealing list of medicinal evidence. The tea can be useful for skin problems and is used in combinations with other lymphatic cleansers like cleavers and dock. The flowers and leaves also contain flavonoids that can help balance hormone problems. Dried flower heads can also be blended and used as a flour extender. The roots were the main event for aboriginal peoples as they stored well and could be steamed later on.

Yellow or curly docks are a survival food that seem to grow all over the West Coast. They are pretty easy to recognize, and leaves and roots are edible, though need boiling and water changing to become tasty, but worth knowing.

Seeds

Seed collecting, as a means of filling your belly on a cold day, sounds promising when we see the great long list of edible seeds around us. However it does shrivel the hopes a bit when we look at the work involved in extracting seeds in enough bulk to make them equal the calories used. Still, it never hurts to know a few things.

We buy pine nuts in the store and pay good dollars for them, but where the heck do they come from? It turns out that pine nuts are the seed that is tucked under the alligator like flaps on all pine cones (don't you love trick questions?) and all pine nuts are edible. We merely seek out the largest ones to eat. Campers are all familiar with squirrels ripping cones apart and tossing the bits down onto their heads, and this is exactly what they are after, too. If you find cones on the ground, lay them near the edge of a fire to dry and open them up to see the little seeds hiding inside. Pine seeds hold lots of oil and go rancid fast, so eat them right away. And by the way, the monkey puzzle tree has some pretty decent sized seeds as well. And when you try to retrieve them, you'll understand the name of this tree better.

Greens

I once had my children's class do an experiment. When they stepped out of the car into my weedy parking area, we had to stop, look down, and identify the plants we were standing on top of. This is what we found: Plantain, hawksbeard, wood sorrel, dandelion, prunella, and sheep sorrel. Okay, I never weed. But the point is that all of this stuff could be picked and eaten. We tasted some on the spot, and then, this being late February, we picked a little bundle of these leaves and headed for another area. It was a bit early for nettle, and the miner's lettuce was just sprouting, but the violets were leafy enough to pluck from, and the ox-eye daisy leaves, which are strangely sweet, were just getting big enough to nibble. We munched our way up to the porch. I got the kids some plates and forks, and tossed the remaining leaves in a colander. I redistributed what was now apparently a salad onto the plates, and to make it more real I added some salad dressing. The kids stared at their plates and poked and tasted a bit. Yuck! It was much more desirable right out of the garden!

There are some wild greens that can be discovered by accidentally mashing them with your boot on a forest path. If a plant smells like onion, or smells like mint, it is a reasonable bet you have found a native wild patch of these, and can use them in your dinner or teapot.

Raw

Just like in your veggie garden, spring is the best time for greens of any kind. Give them a nibble and see how you like them plain. Some leaves, like the violet, are nondescript in terms of taste and a bit tough, but the leaves are small and blend into a salad well. Miner's lettuce is like any bland lettuce. As a rule, younger, smaller, paler leaves are more tender and sweet, so watch where you are picking from the plant. Taste a new young leaf and an old, lower one from the same plant to test this for yourself. When you begin blending things together, you'll discover what you like, what you need to chop small so that its taste is not too overwhelming, and what needs picking young. Ox-eye leaves get chewy when they're bigger and older and when certain plants like dandelion get too big, they are almost inedible.

And Cooked

And many wild plants are just always too bitter for our modern tastes. I am sure these bitter constituents had value for early nibblers, by forcing secretion of more bile and stomach acids, which then broke down and released food values more efficiently. We would still get the same advantages, but we are less likely these days to force ourselves to eat this way, and the truth is that many beneficial food plants are also tough and astringent.

For example, dandelion greens get a lot of press, but they get bitter fast. One trick is to throw a cardboard box or a leafy branch over a healthy dandelion plant. In a few days it will be a lot paler, and consequently easier to eat. This is called blanching and is used for fancy things like Belgian endive and leeks. If leaves of any kind are still bitter, boil them in water, toss the water out and refill, and boil again. Some foods need repeated boiling, but this is obviously only useful when you are truly in a survival situation and have lots of water and fuel.

Berries

I left the most obvious for last. Most of us already recognize a great many berries that grow all around us much of the summer. We could be learning some more, and beginning to learn how to incorporate them into our lives.

When I step through a gate to do an edible consultation, most people are surprised when I tell them, without walking the garden, that they have at least five types of berry growing there. The native salal, salmonberry, thimbleberry, huckleberry and native blackberry are pretty ubiquitous on the West Coast, and many of us also have wild strawberry, Oregon grape, and the double edged presence of the Himalayan blackberry. Some are lucky enough to have blueberry, bunchberry, wild currants and gooseberry. Some areas host hawthorne, Saskatoons, juniper and wild raspberries. Suffice it to say that if you could recognize all the edible berries in your area, you would have access to natural sugars, bio-flavonoids and Vitamin C.

Raw

Most berries don't make it into the kitchen. They are the ideal snacking food. For walks or gardening, it is refreshing to reach out and spend a few minutes gobbling berries before picking up the walking stick or shovel again. Some berries aren't as sweet as others by nature, and some have to be quite ripe to be palatable. Wait for berries like salal to get that dusty look before eating them. And don't forget to experiment by tasting berries at various stages of ripeness so you will be better at picking.

Jam

Although some of the wild berries are not as sweet as the black-berry and raspberry, you can make a decent jam in the same manner as always, by boiling down the berries and mixing in enough sweetener of any variety that the result will be palatable poured over toast or a pancake. Mountain ash berries, salal and Oregon grape berries are all better as a jam than a raw berry.

Fruit

Although crabapples and Indian plums show up on the wild edible lists, I have never seen them in the bush around here. Certainly, there are a lot of red elder berries, and these, although listed as mildly toxic in our local books, were used by native

---

Survivors

That's us (give or take a few weeks of pre-fattening and research.)

Okay, I admit it. I'm one of the nine people in British Columbia who have never watched Survivor. I heard all about it in the lunchroom at work though, and it made me wonder how I would do if I had to live for a couple of days in the woods. So I actually wandered down my driveway with an empty stomach and sat in the trees, just for effect. After a moment of meditation and stomach gurgling, the following truisms hit me:

I should have studied up on this a little sooner. Yup, I should have spent time throughout each change in season, walking around with a savvy friend, learning what each plant looked like at different times of the year — before it became in issue. And instead of memorizing Latin names out of a book, I should learn each plant by taste, leaf size, growth habit and part used. Learning slowly and thoroughly would give me more excuses to get to know my forest, and I'd be less likely to make mistakes in an emergency.

I can't remember everything, so if I get lost, I better do it with a copy of *Plants of Coastal British Columbia (including Washington, Oregon and Alaska)*, *Food Plants of Coastal First Peoples* or *Basic Essentials: Edible Wild Plants and Useful Herbs*. Also a Swiss Army knife, a pot for boiling some of these plants, a water source and some matches, and maybe this article.

Berries — These are the easiest to spot of the available foods, and there is something in fruit through most of the late spring and summer. Of these, the most recognizable are blackberries, huckleberries, strawberries, blueberries, salmon and thimbleberries, salal berries, and Oregon grape fruits. Fruit of the red elderberry and ↗

---

people because they knew they had to be cooked to be safely eaten. Arbutus fruit are edible but not as tasty as fruit we are used to. Rosehips are abundant in fall and although not resembling a fresh mango in the least, can be eaten raw right off the plant. Just gouge out the little hairs and seeds in the center, first. Rosehips soften after a frost, are high in Vitamin C, and are easy to dry for later use in tea.

Weird-looking Bits

There is a lot more out there to eat that is hard to describe, but are worthy foods, especially if we were in need. The Sumac cluster of loose little flowers, called a fruit, can be dried and ground as flour. The leaves can be cooked and eaten in a pinch.

mountain ash can only be eaten after cooking. Carry your plant identification book for the other ones.

Leaves — There are several leafy plants that are easy to recognize. Practice on chickweed, very fresh wild strawberry leaves, young plantain, lamb's quarters, Siberian miner's lettuce, the violet family, dandelion and wood sorrel.

You can also make a pot of nourishing tea from blackberry leaves, rose hips and leaves, or St John's wort. If you come across something that smells like mint, it probably is so throw it in the pot.

Stems — Try these for a bit of bulk. Cut sections of the youngest looking stems of salmon berry, thimbleberry or thistle, (oops — better pack gloves with fingertips if you're planning to get lost) peel the thin bark off, and eat fresh or boiled. The same can be done with the very young peeled shoots of blackberry. If they taste too acidic or bitter for you, like everything else, boil them and discard the water until they are palatable. And if you can tell the difference between burdock and dock, try some very young peeled dock stem, although the burdock won't hurt you.

Others — While you're boiling up a pot of water, try tossing in the roots of thistle, cinquefoil (silverweed), clover, bracken, burdock and fern. And don't be afraid to munch away on the flowers of clover, violet, miner's lettuce and wild roses. There are lots more edible plant parts out there, as well as many mushrooms, and hopefully this will be a starting off point to some learning and chewing that will make you feel safer and more in tune with your local forest. (That darn abundance — it's everywhere!)

Admittedly, a few days of the above diet would leave most North Americans hungry for *real* food, but we would all step out of the bush with cleaner complexions and leaner tummies. And then we could apply to be on Survivor.

The inner bark of almost every native tree was considered food to many indigenous groups, including that of pine, hemlock, cedar, fir, spruce and alder (the alder had to be dried — they knew that). The maple tree gives the obvious sap, if we knew how to access it, but the flower clusters and sprouted seeds are also considered completely edible.

Alder catkins can be cooked up in a pinch, and the tree also has an edible sap.

Mushrooms

There is much to be gleaned in the way of mushrooms, in terms of adding succulent tidbits to meals. Unfortunately, this little handbook is not the place for the great identification details you would need to hike bravely and confidently off to that particular feast. Still, for those with time to learn, the benefits of adding this food to your list of foods is great. On my property, I have identified shaggy manes, black morels and puffball — all reasonably safe to identify — and I know there are more edibles than that and I will slowly learn them. But mistakes have been made by eager neophytes, so I will merely say that you should find someone who absolutely does not take risks, and have them show you some basic mushrooms, name the parts, discuss the toxic look-alikes, and you should get good at finding and eating only when your ability grows.

And once you are the happy recipient of a bag of damp, rich smelling mushrooms, try the simple method of dusting the biggest bits of forest duff off them, slicing them into a sizzling pan

Once you begin gleaning wild foods from your property or local wild space, a shocking truth will hit you — for instance, that although renewable, the food supply is seasonally finite. Once you, your uncle Bob and a local deer or three have gone through a patch, it's over for the time being. And that doesn't include the raccoons and birds who depend on these foods for survival, because let's face it, we have a choice between the woods and the local supermarket and they don't. The aboriginal people dealt with this by farming stands of wild foods so they would yield well. They knew they couldn't over-harvest without harming next year's food supply, I have a funny feeling those measured sensibilities will not survive a modern food crisis. The ethics of how much to take from wild places is a big discussion. If we are truly hungry, we will merely take what we need, and ethics will go out the window. However, approaching your garden walks with an eye to long-term sustainability will make you an aware and careful consumer.

of butter and flipping them about a bit with a dash of pepper. If there are too many to eat and you don't want to risk rotting them by putting them in the fridge, slice them and put them up high in a warm room, and they will dry very easily. When you want them for dinner, put a handful of pieces in a bowl and pour some hot water over them, and in no time, they are ready to throw into the sauce.

I knew, when I took this chapter on, that a few pages would never compare with the detailed, illustrated books I have on my bookshelf. My hope was to get you started!

Hopefully this chapter will:

* Remind the reader that we are surrounded by potential food.
* Give tips for learning to recognize and sample new plant foods.
* Increase confidence in experimenting so that wild gleaning will become a more natural act.
* Get readers familiar with the tastes of the wild.
* Introduce a list of easy to recognize plants to begin learning with.
* Make readers more likely to develop a long-term interest in the edible wild — it is, after all, right outside.

Things to Try and Do

1. Buy at least one good wild food book to have at home as a reference.
2. Learn at least ten new wild plants in the next month.
3. Plan one outing with friends to identify wild plants.
4. Harvest and taste at least one new wild plant a week for a month. Mark it on your calendar.
5. Find at least one plant food that you can learn to store for later use.

Resources

Arora, David. *All That the Rain Promises, and More...A Hip Pocket Guide to Western Mushrooms.* Berkeley: Ten Speed Press, 1991.

A lovely, fun and very informative look at the strange and delicious species often found lurking in our own nearby forests. This book is fully illustrated to help you with identifying species of mushroom and it will fit nicely into your pocket. When hiking in the spring, keep it close at hand!

Couplan, Francois. *The Encyclopedia of Edible Plants of North America*. New Canaan, Keats Publishing, 1998

An ethnobotanist, Couplan digs into his far-reaching knowledge of wild plants to compile this book, which he wrote over a period of twenty-five years. Listing information for around 4,000 plant varieties, the book looks at techniques for harvesting and preparation and includes information about edible plants along with which plants contain healing properties.

Pojar, Jim and MacKinnon, Andy. *Plants of Coastal British Columbia (including Washington, Oregon and Alaska)* Vancouver: Lone Pine Publishing, 1994.

For plant identification, this book is a must. It includes detailed descriptions, photos and histories of just about every forest plant you will find in local forests in this part of North America.

Turner, Nancy J. *Food Plants of Coastal First Peoples*. Vancouver: UBC Press, 1995.

Specific to plants found along the coast of British Columbia, this book includes more than one hundred plants used by Native peoples. It is an important book for those wanting to know more about the history and culture of the first peoples in relation to the harvesting and preparation of these indigenous plants.

CHAPTER 11

By the Sea —
We Shall See
What's on the Seashore
(And Then We'll Eat It)

One woman's meat certainly does look like another one's poison. I know I was pretty surprised the first time I was told that all that stuff laying along the beach was food — the stringy seaweed, the knobbly and strange shells, the limpets and sucking clams. This scene did not elicit squeals of pleasure or hand twisting, eye rolling joy — I was raised to think that this was the kind of stuff you tried not to get on your shoes. But naturally, every culture that has matured by the ocean knows that an amazing amount of this stuff is not only tasty (in the right hands) but nutritious, and maybe delicious. And I had a lot to learn. This was yet another epiphany of late — that many of us would starve in our own environments, unaware that we were surrounded by healthy foods, and knowing full well that other cultures lived for centuries on this very land.

So I wandered down to the ocean and sat on a log and looked at all that plant and animal life stuck to rocks and tucked down in the sand and wafting in the rolling tide, and realized I would have to break this all down into some type of system so I could learn to appreciate it better. But not so strangely, when I got home and opened up my books, that work had all been done for me.

So, just for fun, let's break the ocean foods into groups, such as crustaceans (easy to remember because they all have "crusts" and jointed legs), the mollusks or molluscs (which, just to mess with your head, also generally have crusty shells, but no legs), the seaweeds and the fish. Notice that the subgroup "chocolate" is completely absent. This could be one of my problems.

This chapter will make certain environmentalists very nervous. The idea of hoards rushing to the seashore and tearing up intertidal zones will make their hair stand on end. (Or, even more on end, sea edges are already under huge threat from pollution and harvesting.) If you NEED ocean food please watch your boots in these fragile places, do not rake, shovel, and plunder anything you don't need to bother, take only as much as you need, and return the shells and roots where you found them.

Eating Oceanside Foods

For this section on eating shellfish, I visited one of our local Hot Young Chefs, Ananda Howitt who works at the Gumboot Bistro. I asked him what forlorn hungry folk could do in a crisis if confronted with a food packed beach and a few condiments. As he tossed pots, jostled pans and rushed from stove to chopping block, he told me the following. First, he thought this was a pretty easy situation. He agreed that just about everything found at the ocean front was good food, except jellyfish and sea urchins, which are easy to identify but hard to prepare. (Some cultures dry and salt their jellyfish, or serve it julienned in Vietnamese seafood salad — the sea urchins must come from very cold ocean water and harvesters must know how to remove the ovaries — a skill not usually on the list of a neophyte scavenger. These sounded like foods for better experienced ocean harvesters.) And Ananda mentioned the old problem of pollution, and we decided that hungry people might gobble down something full of water-borne pollutants if there was a food crisis, but that obviously harvesting from isolated areas rather than near marinas and populated areas would be a good plan. He reminded me that the bivalves (two-shelled) critters have a red tide period on the West Coast and that might make us careful about eating them if we couldn't get reports on this, as red tide can be fatal. But he did, while racing through the steam and flames, think that anyone with a stash of garlic and white wine would do fine in this situation. (Note to self: Don't drink all the white wine right after the earthquake.) Ananda tossed my carefully divided list of crustaceans and molluscs out the window and said they were all good with garlic and white wine, and we are both hoping like crazy you have put some cooking oil away to coat the grill with. We realized there will be no lemons during a crisis, but Ananda told me a recipe of using thyme, clean Sumac flowers, sesame, and ending with salt, in that quantitative order, as a replacement for lemons. (Note: Oh yes, and don't eat all the sesame seeds right after the earthquake.) He also reminded me that liquorice root and fennel seed were great with seafood.

A quick hot sear in the beginning, followed by a slow cook on low heat after flipping would be a proper Rule of Thumb for most seafood. He noted, as he frisbee'd a loaded plate towards the server, who caught it with a deft elbow bend and headed out the door, that all seafood should be thoroughly cooked unless you absolutely know how fresh it is. If you just pulled it out of the water, this is not such an issue. All these critters can be kept nicely in a bucket of cold seawater, all the better for the ones that squirt out sand and effluent for the first few hours of capture. Critters such as mussels and clams can be steamed right in

> **Crustaceans:** Lobsters, shrimp, prawns, barnacles, crabs, crayfish (mostly things that can run away but could be trapped). **Mollusks (Molluscs):** Abalone, clam, oyster, geoduck, conch, cockle, mussel, whelk, limpets, periwinkle, scallops (mostly things that can't run away but you would have to get really wet to scoop up).

your metal bucket of salt water on fire, but he reserved the oyster as something he would bake dry on a rack. He mentioned that garden herbs like rosemary, thyme and oregano would really perk up these ocean foods, and reminded me that dry herbs should be added early in the cooking to give them time to rehydrate and infuse the cooking medium, while fresh herbs should be added last to release their goodness at the very end. He said everybody knows that. Ha ha.

▬ Al's Oysters ▬▬▬▬▬▬▬▬▬▬▬▬▬▬▬▬▬▬

Al can't believe that something this tasty can be eaten in an emergency, and he even has a barbecue right outside.

Ingredients

Oysters, butter, garlic, parmesan cheese, Tabasco sauce.

Hold oyster firmly in left hand (or right hand if you are left-handed). Use a rag or leather glove to grip oyster shell. Stick screwdriver into "muscle" and twist sideways. Lay opened oysters on the barbecue rack, pour on garlic butter, sprinkle with parmesan cheese and a few drops of Tabasco sauce. Can be cooked to any point, but until the flesh is solid is sufficient.

Seaweed

Seaweed is slowly regaining a place in our diet and so it should. It's full of nutrients, is pretty easy to find in stores and even easier on your local beach. We can learn to recognize the more commonly eaten sea vegetables like bull kelp, ocean lettuce, nori (*Porphyra*) and kombu (*Laminaria*), but all of them are potential food, fresh or dried. Let's take nori as an example. In his book, *Pacific Seaweeds*, Louis Druehl points out that nori is probably one of the healthiest foods in the world, making it an excellent survival food. It is rich in carbohydrates, proteins and vitamins, and grows throughout the year high on the beach where we can easily harvest it. Nori and other seaweeds can be added to stews, soups, stirfrys, rice or beans. It holds enough salt to deepen the taste of your dishes. Better yet, Louis points out that seaweed can be used to wrap fish and potatoes that will be cooked in hot coals, replacing the need for tinfoil. Leftovers can be scattered onto the garden or stirred into the manure teapot to release their hoard of nutrients there.

Fish

Poor fish. We haven't eaten them all up yet, but we're doing our best (or worst). It's unfortunate that they are so luscious, even baked over a fire with garden herbs and a dab of oil, although in a condiment-rich situation, things will look even better. The trick with fish is to cook it through without burning it on the bottom, and this could mean wrapping it in strong foil or seaweed, baking it in a covered pot, or making soup out of it. But just like the Japanese have shown us, raw fish, very fresh, sliced very thin, is something a few of us could adapt to (Ananda suggests salmon, tuna, small flounder, sea bass, red snapper, tilapia, deep sea shrimp or sweet shrimp, scallops, oysters, squid and cuttlefish for this). And while you're learning to clean a fish, don't forget the other name for fish roe is caviar!

Now we know why our shore-dwelling friends look so healthy and smug!

Resources

Website

Fisheries and Oceans Canada, "Red Tide PSP and Contamination," pac.dfo-mpo.gc.ca/recfish/PSP&contamination_e.htm (accessed April 11, 2008).

Book

Druehl, Louis. *Pacific Seaweeds: A Guide to Common Seaweeds of the West Coast*, Pender Harbour, BC: Harbour Publishing, 2001.

This is a very readable book with great line drawings as well as photographs. It includes information on lifecycles, ecology and nutrient content, and several usable recipes.

Snively, Gloria. *Exploring the Seashore in British Columbia, Washington and Oregon: A Guide to Shorebirds and Intertidal Plants and Animals*. Vancouver: Gordon Soules Book Publishers, 2003.

This book contains detailed line drawings of the many creatures, great and small, to be found on a beach, plus habitat descriptions. There are also many photos and coastal maps. This is one of those "you'll only need this one book" books.

CHAPTER 12

The 18 Minute Medic: Quick Medicine, at Your Door

Maybe you're up at the cabin, you've whacked yourself on the thigh with your mattock and it looks like it's getting infected. Or perhaps the Big One has finally hit and you're cut and sore and cannot get back into your house for your first aid kit. Maybe you've been walking on the beach and have a freely bleeding wound from a buried chunk of prehistoric beer bottle. What to do when you cannot get help on the double?

It is good to learn right about now that our forests and gardens are full of intriguing medicinal plants. But how come so many plants have qualities that are beneficial to humans? The scientists say it's just a coincidence — that we are all made up of oxygen and nitrogen and carbon, just in different proportions, and we all have to confront the same health issues of aging and virus attack. Plants actually have the lucky break, as they are loaded with constituents that support body systems, both theirs and ours. Some prevent oxidation of cells, some stun insects who bite into their leaves (and we thought we were the smart, highly evolved ones), some plants ward off bacteria and kill viruses, some stop bleeding and the scientists are working to untangle the uses of literally thousands more of the active constituents.

However, while they toil away in the lab, we can still be happily using these plants to our benefit. Humans have known for centuries that particular herbage will perform given duties for them, and science can now back this up. The ancient Celts took borage to make them brave in battle. Did they know it was an adrenal stimulant? Tribes in South America knew which plants fought infection and which ones brought huge awareness. Meanwhile the people further north had been gathering and storing medicinals for centuries. The Chinese have been documenting plant medicines for literally thousands of years, which are now being discovered (Land sakes, what makes us so proud to finally figure it out?) to be as fully functional and effective as they were written to be in ancient writings.

Although some plants are complex and it is difficult to draw their medicines out, many are in fact simple to use, easy to find and identify, and are essentially harmless in terms of doing ourselves injury. It is wise to know a handful of plants that can get us out of trouble, either while we are waiting for help to arrive or as a longer term assist in a sticky situation.

What are the problems we are likely to run into in times of food crises? What will our medical needs be? There is a cheery thought! We would assume in the case of an earthquake the problem of bleeding may arise, with the possibility of infection from broken glass or ragged metal. There is the problem of reducing inflammation in bruises or fractures. We may need help in improving digestion of strange foods. We may get belly and bowel upsets from food that is going off, or bad water. There is the need for a calm head and an easy sleep.

And how do we get these medicines into our body? The most obvious answer is to eat the plants or imbibe them in tea. The next most obvious answer is to mash them up and apply them directly to wounds. After that come the tinctures and salves, but we are going to stick with handy plants that can be used quickly.

It's a good idea, when learning about healing plants, to either track down a knowledgeable person who can give you good samples and show you around, or to find excellent plant identification books, and to just follow directions, ma'am, when putting new things into your body. We are all different and some folks may react badly to a plant that would not hurt others. However, I am not going to spend too much time on warnings for this list of plants, because I have seen the list of chemicals in children's breakfast cereals and I want to keep my fear (and yours) in proportion.

Calendula: This is a pretty little plant that wants no care, will grow on a sandy beach, will flower all summer and heal your wounds as well. It is anti-fungal, anti-inflammatory, useful for burns and rashes, helps stop bleeding, speeds wound healing, and stimulates bile, which helps digest foods properly. Calendula shouldn't be taken internally during pregnancy, but is still great on the skin for cuts and rashes.

Cayenne pepper: Buy a packet of cayenne at the health food store and keep it in the cupboard, or fill an old film canister with it and keep it in your first aid kit. Cayenne will stop a bleeding wound, relieve toothache and can relieve painful joints. It can be blended with plantain in a poultice to draw out slivers and other foreign bodies. Just remember not to touch your eyes and face after applying it.

Chickweed (*Stellaria spp.*): This is a famous spring tonic for bringing vitamins into our body, but also an easily recognized anti-inflammatory medicine. Throw a bundle over your sore eyes, press a bunch of leaves to a sting. Drink a strong tea of this all day to act as a laxative or help with the inflammation of cystitis.

Comfrey (*Symphytum officinale*): This is famous for its ability to heal wounds as it contains allantoin that helps with cell division. Every home or common property should have one of these big showy plants around (just keep cutting the flowering tops off for the compost, if you want to keep the baby plants from running amok). Comfrey leaves are prickly to the touch, however, smashed up with some warm water and laid over a wound, this plant can help with sprains and traumatic injuries and, used over the long term, undisplaced broken bones. In addition, it is especially good for awkward breaks like toes and ribs. The root can even be ground up and poulticed to relieve the inflammation of hemorrhoids. Just cut a section of root out at any time of year, scrub off any soil and the damp rootbark, mash the root as well as you can under the circumstances, and apply it to the wounded spot with a damp cloth over it.

Garlic: Disaster has struck and you absolutely can't get your heart medication prescription filled? Well, get a load of this, high quantities of garlic (three to six crushed cloves per day) will reduce blood pressure and cholesterol levels, reduce the risk of thrombosis, and lower blood sugar. Not only that, garlic is a broad range antibiotic with anti-histamine properties. It helps with skin infections *and* is great in hummus. I tell you, you can't lose with this plant. For those of you looking at that puny shriveled thing in the net bag you bought last month, get serious. Start buying bags from the farmers' market instead or grow it yourself. Use it all the time whether you need it or not. Put it in soups, eggs, stir frys and salad dressings. Maybe if you take enough of it, you won't need those prescriptions. Please note that garlic may cause heartburn in pregnant women, and may upset the tummies of babies ingesting garlic-laden breast milk, but heck, you don't need to worry about the vampires!

Honey: This one is not an herb, but another magic medium. Honey will keep forever in the back of a cupboard (heck, it kept in the back of a pyramid for thousands of years) and is another ancient healer that's working its way back into the books. It is antibacterial; speeds wound healing, and can be applied directly to cleaned wounds or applied to gauze, which is then placed on the wound. Very old and serious wounds like diabetic ulcers are being found to heal quickly with daily applications of honey. It also acts as a physical barrier to grime if you can't keep a wound area clean, for instance if you must work around infectious mediums and have no bandages. Honey is easier to apply if it is warm, or you may want to dilute it a bit. Honey is also excellent taken for sore throats, upset stomachs and irregular bowels. So remember to be nice to those bees! Never give honey to children under the age of two — it could incite a botulism outbreak in their gut.

Lemon balm (*Melissa officinalis*): Well known as a gentle mood relaxer, drink a few cups of this herb throughout the day to take the edge off anxiety and stress. Lemon balm is good for stomach spasms that occur when we eat bad food or have a tummy bug and is safe for helping get kids off to sleep. Its mild antiviral properties make it good for feverish colds, and it may also be used as a poultice to relieve shingle pain. And, it's so terribly easy to grow that people rip it out of their gardens.

Peppermint (*Mentha spp.*): This is my secret weapon against Norwalk virus, that nasty bug that causes such bad gut pain. Even a single cup of good strong peppermint tea can help the awful spasms of a bellyache, and can also help with basic digestion upset from eating new (or too much) food. This herb can help with nausea and headaches. I have not tried using it as a poultice but it's said to help with painful joints. Don't give to young babies.

Plantain (*Plantago spp.*): Yet another overlooked little miracle plant, plantain is easy to find and recognize. This is my favorite poultice leaf, for tugging off the plant, mashing with the back of a knife and putting quickly onto a fresh wound. It's excellent for bangs, bruises and burns, for infections and abscesses, stings and slow-to-heal wounds. Or you can make tea from it for internal problems such as diarrhea, or try it for when you're stuck for something to relieve symptoms of asthma or hay fever.

St. John's wort (*Hypericum perforatum*): Most know this herb for its ability to soothe anxiety and nervous exhaustion. It even works for PMS! You can use the top few inches with flowers and leaves in a tea, or try the oil infusion for burns or nerve pain.

If you are fair of complexion and drink a lot of St. John's wort, avoid being in bright sunlight. Also, if you are already on a mood shifting medication, either take one or the other, but not both. St. John's is one of those herbs that can interact with many prescription medications, but certainly if you have run out of the factory made stuff and would like something to relieve stressful feelings, try drinking a tea of this plant.

Thyme (*Thymus spp.*): This is another culinary plant we should be buying a flat of and taking home to the warmest, fastest draining parts of our gardens. Thyme is great on pizza and tomato dishes, but is also both antiviral and antibacterial. Drink lots of this tea for upper respiratory infections. It is said to be good for diarrhea as well.

Yarrow (*Achillea millefolium*): The Romans took this herb with them into battle in order to staunch bleeding, so there has been lots of time to test its qualities as a blood-stopping poultice. It's a good plant to have in the garden for fresh use right on a wound, and if you have a household full of active children who cut themselves a lot, you might want to preserve a clump for winter use as well. Yarrow dries up lots of other fluids besides bleeding wounds and the tea can be used for runny noses or allergies, and is good for feverish colds. Try inhaling over a bowl of it in warm water for hay fever. In addition, it is a bitter, so it will help you digest foods. Use it lightly if you are pregnant.

All these plants grow easily in the Lower Mainland of BC and Northwestern United States, and all can be easily dried (or in the case of garlic, cured and bagged for winter) for use at any time of year. These plants have very little to no side effects, most can be given to children, and, my favorite of all is they don't cost any money beyond the first purchase of plants. Many of these are harvestable through many months of the year and keep well in many forms (tea, tincture or infused oil) for later use. It is good to know your local herbs because, as our earthquake guy Bill says, if, or rather *when* (he never says "if"—he only says "when") there is an earthquake, it could take two or three weeks for householders in outlying areas to receive any kind of help. Hospitals will be swamped and staffed by personnel who have their own problems at home. Do what you can to look after yourself.

So what is the best method for getting these herbs into action? You can heat most herbs in water for a tea, or apply them directly to a wound. Herbs definitely have a "best" time of day and month to be harvested for medicine (and that is usually late morning to mid day on a dry day, and usually just before flowering) but for an emergency, just pick the herb at any time. It will still have active constituents — just not in the highest possible dose.

> **RoseMarie's Cold and Allergy Tea**
>
> (She says it's good for snoring too)
>
> Blend as many of these in a teapot as you can find: Peppermint, sage, rosemary, thyme and perilla. Pour boiled water over this and allow to steep for at least ten minutes.

Infusion: This is how to make any good tea. Plant parts, either fresh or dried, are put in a container, water that has just been boiled is poured over it, the lid is put on and it is allowed to steep for at least ten minutes. More is better. Drink lots to be sure you are getting a therapeutic dose.

Poultice: The easiest form of poultice is merely smashed leaves laid directly over the injured spot. Plantain is fabulous for this, and I keep plenty around, because I live alone up a dirt road, and I use lots of big heavy tools. Recently when I banged myself on the hand with a pickax, immediately after politely whispering "darn" under my breath, I grabbed a handful of plantain leaves, smacked them against the fence with the flat side of the pick ax blade, and wrapped them around my sore hand. Then I sat pathetically under the raspberry bushes and listened to the bees buzz for a while, then looked sadly at my hand. It still hurt like hell, but there was very little resulting bruising (making it deadly hard to get any sympathy from my friends later) and healed very quickly. If you have the time to rinse the herbs and lay them over some gauze, this is good too, but in a pinch, know your blood and bruise control herbs and have them near the house.

Infused Oils: Winter does happen, making fresh herbs impossible to access. Many medicinal constituents will dissolve into warm oil, and can be kept safely into the next year. The oil, poured onto a cloth, is also a good way to apply medicine to bruises, sprains and cuts.

The best and quickest way to make an oil infusion is to get a big handful of clean leaves of the plant you may need (plantain, calendula, comfrey) and mash the leaves up as well as you can. Put this material in the bottom of a glass bread pan or a jar with a lid, and cover with cooking oil, so that no tip is exposed to the air. Put this in bright sunlight or on the lip of the woodstove — somewhere where it will get consistent heat for as long as you can manage it. I put my jars in paper bags in the sun, and bring them in at night. Some infusions can be filtered through a coffee filter in only a few hours such as chickweed and plantain, while others like St. John's wort flower can take days to weeks of adding newly picked flowers before filtering and bottling. Where the books say to use a yogurt maker to get the desired, consistent heat, this is not always possible and we have to remember that infused oils were successfully made long before electricity and the yogurt maker (and even coffee filters) were invented. My St. John's wort oil achieves a good rich red shade using old-fashioned sunlight.

▬ Recipe for St. John's wort infused oil ▬▬▬▬

You will only have a few weeks in summer to make this oil, so when you see the first flowers opening on your local St. John's plants, fill a clean small jar with organic cooking oil and gently pick the buds and open flowers into the oil. Put the lid on and put this jar in a sunny window. Pick more flowers over the coming days and weeks (but wait til rain or dew has evaporated to keep water out of your oil) and keep adding them to the jar. You can help things by mashing your flowers up with a fork or popping them in a blender. When the oil is a good rich red, filter the flowers out with a coffee filter and put the jar away in a cool place, to use on burns and inflammations.

Tincture: Tinctures are not too practical in terms of emergency medicine, unless you are brilliant enough to meticulously plan your injuries for about two weeks after starting a batch. Tinctures are the form of plant medicine that results when we soak the mashed plant in strong alcohol, shake it every day, and filter it into a bottle. Then we would have the plant medicine available to us for years. A successful rule of thumb would be to stick the well-identified herb into your blender, or chop it into small bits, put it into a very clean little jar, and add vodka until it is covered. Cap and label it, and shake it every day (that you remember) and then two weeks later pour it through a coffee filter. Bottle the clean, filtered liquid, label and date it, taking as needed, which usually translates to a full dropper several times a day. This is not an elegant translation of the best recipes, but will get you something useful. My best tincture story is of the weekend I rubbed my very itchy bug bitten face with my grubby hands after spreading manure all day. The result was one very pink eye, and by that evening, the whole area felt sore and hot right down the side of my nose. Being lazy, I decided to put off the visit to emergency for the next day, and phoned our local animal healer, Val. She said to dilute a few drops of calendula tincture in a tablespoon of warm water and to bathe my eye with that. I did so, falling asleep with a soaked gauze pad over it, and awoke the next morning with not enough symptoms to bother going to the doctor. By the next day, it had cleared completely. I won't recommend not going to a doctor in a book for the public, but if you can't get there, try out your little green friends as a way to avoid more serious problems.

There are hundreds more medicinal plants that grow well and easily all over North America, but this handful will get you through several problems.

Cross-reference Guide

Anxiety: Lemon balm, St. John's wort
Bleeding cuts: plantain, yarrow, thyme, cayenne.
Diarrhea: Plantain, yarrow, thyme, garlic
Indigestion with stomach spasms: Lemon balm, the mints, honey
Infected wounds: Plantain, calendula, lemon balm, honey, comfrey, garlic
Sprains and bruises: Comfrey, calendula, chickweed, plantain

Resources

Website

Plants for a Future: Edible, Medicinal and Useful Plants for a Healthier World, pfaf.org.

This UK charity is compiling a database, which currently houses approximately 7,000 species of plants, and has a medicinal category for each plant, with a fabulous cross reference database for searching for plants by the healing properties they contain.

Books

Cech, Richo. *Making Plant Medicine*. Williams, OR: Horizon Herbs, 2000.

The most well thumbed of my plant medicine books, this contains very well explained recipes for all sorts of medicines, medicinal uses of individual plants and great stories of Richo's own experiences. Very readable and a wonderful resource for many levels of herbal use.

Ody, Penelope. *The Complete Medicinal Herbal: A Practical Guide to the Healing Properties of Herbs, with More Than 250 Remedies for Common Ailments*. Toronto: Key Porter Books, 1997

Another fave and great for the beginner, for its wonderful graphics, simple quick reference layout, case studies and photos of medicine making techniques.

CHAPTER 13

Water

A funny thing happened during a month of nasty weather in Vancouver, British Columbia, in 2006. Heavy rains had caused turbidity in the local reservoir, and the health department had posted a "boil water" advisory. Although this seemed fairly straightforward, and although the water was still testing fine, and no one had actually gotten sick, it caused a lot of fear. Instead of boiling their water, many people lined up in the pouring rain at grocery stores and competed over the limited supply of bottled water that was available. There was tension and arguments as supplies ran out. Our normally sane town quite quickly changed into a place where fingers were pointed, news was twisted and the bottled water folk were very happy. The funny thing happened, as legend has it, when a young child pointed out the window at the still thrashing rain and said, "Hey, Mommy, why don't we just drink that?"

This short-lived event made me worry about what would happen in an earthquake — our *thinking* mechanism would go right out the window. It is good to run through a few scenarios beforehand so that if something happened fairly fast to separate us from our tap, our hindbrains would run forward with these thoughts:

Water Collection Should be Part of Our Lives

Yup, sorry, but that water running out of our taps is the same stuff that falls out of the sky. It trickles through the watersheds, into reservoirs, and is then filtered. Sometimes it is treated, but it all ends up in big old pipes that come to our houses. This means that we could probably get that water ourselves in large buckets if we wanted, and cut out the four-hundred-and-twelve steps in between. And we would likely feel even less helpless if we knew a few details about water collection.

I have several big food-grade barrels scattered around that collect water off the roof. I mostly use it in my garden while knowing that if I have to, I can flush the toilet, do the dishes or in a pinch, drink the stuff. I was a bit worried about drinking it, because it had to run over roofing shingles to get to my barrels, but my faithful pooch, Cooma, gulped it down without hesitation. Cooma was eleven years old when we moved here, slowing down and developing a heart condition. I figured that if drinking this water would shorten her life, it was not a long way to go. She drank this water almost exclusively. Then I ran out of money for her heart meds and put her on herbs, and later, a healthier diet. She kicked the heart condition, gulped down that water some more, and lived to sixteen-and-a-half — not a bad age for a fifty pound dog. My guess is that the roof run-off didn't shorten her life too much.

Methods for getting water

Well, it does fall out of the sky all winter, so this would be a good time to collect it.

Find a food-grade barrel and place it under a section of roof (I'm voting for the metal clad wood-shed roof for my own drinking water). Look around for a greenhouse, shed or your house roof; whichever has the most innocuous roof, and then find a piece of down pipe. Setting gutter along a roof is not a difficult thing. Just remember to tilt it slightly downwards, and to clean out any leaves that have collected during the fall. Connect your downspout so that it drains into the barrel, and cut a piece of wood to fit the barrel top to keep critters out. You might want to give this a good cleaning a couple of times a year during a rain so that the systems are clean, and to check that wire filters are cleared and doing their job.

Putting buckets, plastic totes and roasting pans out to catch water during a downpour will certainly work, especially if you have many garden buckets. However, do remember there may be no running water to clean them out at the time of an emergency, so it might be wise to always keep a few clean buckets tucked away for a rainy day. Write "drinking water" on them in black felt pen and do not use them for anything else.

Caught short in the rainy season with no saved water supply, you could pretend you were in the forest and drape some plastic or clean tarp over two poles, and arrange it to funnel down into a collecting bucket to speed up the process.

Careful use of short supplies

When collecting water, remember that you will want to have it for several uses — ultra clean water for drinking and cooking, roof water for bathing and doing dishes, and used water for flushing. When you create systems like this, it gets easier after awhile. Many cultures live this way all the time to save water. We could do it, too, and ease up pressure on our water systems.

When I was living here without running water for a couple of months, I realized that I wanted a pot of warm water on the woodstove at all times. I would first use it to wash my face, and then leave it there so that I could wash my hands quickly during the day. Sometimes I would dampen a cloth to wipe down the counter, and then it would get put in a basin at dinnertime for the dishes or poured into the back of the toilet. I saved the nice sweet well water from Bruce and Doneal's for drinking. It takes a while to get into a good rhythm when your water suddenly shuts off, but remember to save the good stuff to keep you hydrated.

More tips for using way less water

When you don't have much water you learn to sensibly use what's available. Washing food in a basin and doing dishes in a basin uses less water than using the sink, and you can then carry the water down the hall and pour it into the toilet tank. Washing your body out of a basin works too! For quick tooth brushing, put about half-cup of water into your mug, dip your brush into it, and apply the toothpaste to the brush. Brush your teeth, and use half the mug water for two separate swishes and rinses. If three people are going to have a cup of coffee, only boil three cups of water in your pot. Use "middle" quality water for boiling pasta, potatoes, or other foods that you will be draining the water off later, and save the "A" quality water for drinking and for making soups and stews.

As for flushing that toilet, don't forget that urine is a fabulous source of nitrogen for your garden. You can dilute urine and pour it into the compost heap, under the fruit tree or into a manure tea blend. There's no need to waste toilet water! Solid wastes can be deposited into a clean five-gallon bucket, and covered with a layer of soil or wood chips. When this is full or the emergency over, you can put the lid on this bucket and place it behind a convenient tree for a year, when it will be safe to empty out under the hedge.

Learn to Clean Your Water

When we get thirsty, we get cleverer about searching out water sources. However, we have to be careful — our modern tummies don't contain the antibodies they used to, and we can react badly to small amounts of contaminants in the water. This can cause diarrhea or vomiting, both of which will make us even more dehydrated. So, whether we are draining our waterbed into the kettle, dismantling the hot water tank or drinking out of buckets, we'll want to make sure that water is clean before we drink it. And where normally when we clean something, we just get some hot water and... Yes, yes, we don't have any water. And since we do know that our bodies are more susceptible to illness when we're stressed, it's best to take extra good care not to get ill.

Once you have collected some drinking water, you may just want to assume it is contaminated. Melted snow and rainwater are considered clean (if the bucket it is collected in was clean) but groundwater and other sources should be viewed with care.

The two most popular methods for making sure that the water we use is safe for our stomachs is to either boil it or to put bleach or iodine into it.

Boiling

If you have access to fuel, then boiling water hard for a good ten minutes will make it safe. You may not have enough cooking fuel to treat the large amounts of drinking water you may need.

In that case, you can use what is termed a chemical treatment — adding elements that will kill bacteria in water. Some homes already have bleach (5.25% *sodium hypochlorite*) in the laundry room, which can be used, however, check that it doesn't have additives or perfumes. Never use granulated bleach — it's toxic! Some bathrooms still contain bottles of iodine and this can be used in a pinch, although from the sounds of it, it's pretty vile to drink and can't be used by pregnant or nursing women or people with thyroid conditions.

Chemical treatment

Bleach	Clear water	Cloudy water
1 litre/quart	1 drops	4 drops
4 litres/gallon	2 – 4 drops	8 drops
20 litres/5 gallons	11 drops	1 teaspoon
50 gallons	1¾ teaspoon (9 ml)	

Stir well in and let sit for one hour before drinking. The mixture should smell like bleach.

Iodine	Clear Water	Cloudy Water
1 litre/quart	3 drops	6 drops
4 litres/gallon	12 drops	4 drops

And again, stir this together very well. You should be able to smell iodine.

Living on the shadow of a rainforest, there is no excuse for us not to have a personal backup system for water. Maybe we just need more five-year-olds making our big decisions for us.

Notes for Breastfeeding Moms

Maintaining a regular breastfeeding regime may be difficult for a mom who is stressed by an emergency situation. It is important for mothers to be protected and not separated from their babies. Others should handle details so that some form of normalcy can continue. Breastfeeding mothers need good nutrition and plenty of fluids. Breast milk remains the very best food for baby. Unless a mother is unable to breastfeed, a breast milk substitute (infant formula) should not be used — this is particularly true if water quality is questionable.

A highly stressed mom might feel that she has no milk but it is not physically possible to "lose" your milk — it is there, it is only temporarily inhibited; this may last from a few minutes to a few hours. If the mother continues to put the baby to the breast, the milk will return. If you are given a breast milk substitute like formula, drink it yourself or mix it into the family's food.

Things to Do

- Buy some water treatment tablets at your local drugstore and keep them with your camping gear.
- If you use bleach, make sure you have the plain type.
- Tuck away a couple of clean buckets with lids and a large piece of clean plastic for gathering water.
- Either purchase a couple of big plastic camping water carriers, or find a large container with a tight lid that you can still pour from easily. Stored water should be rotated every six months. If you already drink out of the large, refillable plastic bottles, begin buying at least two ahead.

Resources

Provincial Emergency Program, Emergency Management BC (Ministry of Public Safety and Solicitor General), "Individual and Neighbourhood ALL HAZARD Emergency Preparedness Workbook," pep.bc.ca/hazard_preparedness/AllHazards_web .pdf (accessed April 11, 2008).

This workbook is an all-inclusive guide to family emergency planning in the province of British Columbia.

Stevens, James Talmage. *Making the Best of Basics: Family Preparedness Handbook*. Detroit, Michigan: Gold Leaf Press, 1997.

This book covers many homesteading issues that could be used for emergency or low impact living, and has great information on water collection, treating and storage, and will help you figure out how much you have to save for a long term emergency.

CHAPTER 14

I'm Too Busy
Watching "Survivor"
to Live Through a Food Crisis!

My dear friends at work tell me that they don't have time to make an earthquake kit, never mind put in a garden. They have to take Sarah to soccer, and drop Billy at Judo, and shop for a friend's birthday party, and take Foofoo or Fifi (or whatever that darling creature is) to the vet to have its nails clipped. But strangely, they keep the Survivor TV program lottery up to date, and never seem to miss a show. They have time to watch other people survive, yet no time to plan for emergencies. They'll discuss the TV show no end, but haven't shown up for a single earthquake preparedness meeting. My theory is this — talking about surviving an emergency is never fun unless you're imagining sitting next to a buffed prior electronics exec from Chicago named Brian. And you're being filmed, and you're being paid for it. Then it would be pretty interesting.

In my other life in my clearing in the bush, where there are few TV sets, I used to sit around with the locals and talk about survival, except they never called it that, and besides, they had all lived in the country for a good many years and had to have certain skills. Over a few beers and with rain rattling the windows, the old timers would throw storm stories and rampant bears and freak floods around just as other people might trade hockey scores and horror stories of root canals. I did pay attention to the stories — they were intriguing to me — but I never thought I would have to learn from them.

And then: It was late on the night of December 29, 1996.

We had already had an unusual amount of snow for the West Coast, and I was watching the ruler I had shoved into the snow on the railing outside slowly disappear. I was already impatient with the weather, as it had prevented me from doing any food shopping on the way home from work in the previous weeks. I was afraid of being stuck in the snow in the shopping mall parking lot, and hated coming up the long, steep slippery road home in the dark. Besides, I was really busy. Still, I had spent the days both before and since Christmas wishing I had stocked up. My little home up the mountain was low on vitals! I turned on the radio before bed that night and heard the announcer warn of a freak snowstorm. Several feet of the powdery stuff were expected at higher elevations. What did he mean by several feet? I lived at "higher elevations." My first impulse was to run outside and bring in a fresh load of firewood. But then I decided that it never snowed that much here, that radio guy was off his rocker, and I shoved the last two pieces of firewood into my little stove and went off to bed.

I was awoken in a strange twilight by an unfamiliar "kar-ummph" sound that seemed to come from nearby. It woke me enough to ponder on it with a niggling bit of worry. I pulled on my dressing gown, shivered my way down the chilly hall, and looked out my living room window. There was snow all right, lots of it. Feet and feet of it, all right. My truck was a white mound, the greenhouse was nearly invisible, and my woodshed was...gone, a slightly raised hump in a snow-laden wilderness. All my dry wood was down there somewhere. The ax for chopping the roof up was under there somewhere, too. Well, nothing to do about it without a cup of coffee in me. I filled the kettle and made myself a cuppa as I toyed with the logistics of retrieving firewood from under the heavy roof and all that snow when suddenly...click! The lights went out. Darn. No electric power meant no running water, since the pump was hydro driven. Suddenly, I realized I was in one of those funny survival-type situations. I was alone on a hillside in a poorly insulated 45-year-old mobile home, without electricity, running water or easily available firewood, in waist-deep snow — *and I had forgotten to get married!* I hate it when I forget stuff. But I had to put that little oversight away for now, and handle this myself. I had to wade through waist deep snow, hand-dig down to the woodshed roof, pull it apart with my little mittened hands, and retrieve, piece by piece, the precious firewood that would make my house warm.

I did this by making several trips, and was careful to keep my socks dry because I could see ice forming on the inside of the windows even as I worked. I knew I shouldn't let myself get chilled. By noon, I had reloaded the wood box, curtained off the living room to retain heat, had nursed a little fire, and had worked up a ferocious appetite. And I hadn't been shopping in days. But wait! I remembered that Good Old Mom (who we call Sarge) had supplied me with a Care Package for Christmas, and I dug this out from under the bed. Now, this was under the bed, and not in my cupboard, because Sarge frequently forgets my tastes in foods, so the annual Care Package gets tucked way back for true emergencies. And this is what that suddenly precious box offered up: Canned stew, canned soups, instant coffee, and a little tin of mandarin slices, which had seemed insane at the time, but heck! They looked pretty loverly about now.

I melted some snow, cooked up some rice on my little fire and poured the hot stew over it, and had a fine meal. By the second day, completely dehydrated from eating all that canned foods, I ate the luscious little orange slices. It was a good thing I didn't know it would be another twelve days before the water line thawed out, because at that time I was still pretty thirsty. I could have used six cans of that stuff.

I know that I wasn't in any real danger during that snowstorm. I was unlikely to freeze to death, and would have been fine without any food at all, though very hungry. But there were some important lessons for me wrapped up in that few days up the hill. One of them was not to let myself run out of food. And to remember that scary experiences can come anytime, to anybody, very quickly. Then I thought that maybe I should start dating again. But the big lesson for me was about paying attention to radio announcers.

Here are some ways to find lost hours in the day to be food safety conscious.

1. Time the hours a week you spend watching TV. Set a pad of paper and pencil by the set, jot down beginning, and end times for a couple of days. Multiply this by the days in the week, then per month, then for a year. Yes, we know that you only watch high quality documentaries, but still.

2. Use your time on the computer well. Answer all email at 9 PM, or right after work and then turn off your monitor. If you are a Facebookie (a person who spends much of their free time on the social software site called Facebook, either poking friends, or emailing), it is time to figure out your priorities and where you are in the world.

3. Trade errands with friends and relatives who live nearby so that only one of you is picking up children or making cookies for the parent's group.

4. Have your family become more involved in your life. Help each other with daily errands so you all have more time. This will bring you closer together, too.

5. Do as much shopping as you can on the way to or from work so that you have unbroken time to think and plan on the weekends.

6. Plan errands carefully. Watch your calendar and phone ahead to book appointments back-to-back. Shop in loops so that you don't spend time backtracking. Watch for hidden time-wasters. Instead of driving out to return that single video, just pay the extra two dollars and do it when you are nearby. You would have spent that (or more) on gas anyways. That saves the environment, too.

7. Time your phone calls, and see how many you can make that last only two minutes. Stick to the topic and get off the phone.

8. Check into your resistance to emergency planning. Make a list of all the things preventing you from moving ahead with it. You may realize that the bottom line is that you believe others will look after you in a crisis. That's not fair. That makes you a liability. Be an asset so you can help others.

This is a good time to work out your life priorities. Being food secure can be a multi-faceted reward. Fifi's nails and other constant errands that would look strange in an apocalypse may need to be reconsidered. For instance, Fifi's toenails might be worn down by having a steady jog on pavement, and it could be good for you to get out more, too. Saving time in the above ways is not just for emergency planning — we all need more time with family and loved ones. So now that you have carved out some time...

The Ten-Minute Planner

All of the tasks listed below can be finished in ten minutes or less. You could do them while your kettle is boiling, or while waiting for little Jimmy to get out of the bathroom, and so forth.

Spend ten minutes a day completing one of the following:

- Look up your local library on the Internet to get their hours of operation. Learn about ordering books online.
- Order some of the resources I have mentioned throughout this book that interest you.
- Make a list of topics you would like to research for future library visits.
- Make a list of people living nearby that you could discuss Emergency Planning with.
- Make another list of people with whom you could share errands.
- Call your community center and find out where the local farmers markets are.

New Year's Resolutions to Keep!

- Stop talking about it and start learning about simple living skills. Look through the local library for books to read with all that spare time.
- Break out the camping equipment and figure out how long you could cook without running out of fuel.
- Learn about raw food diets.
- Stop waiting for next year to put in a garden, whether it is in the ground, in containers on your patio or in raised beds. If there is available earth, put a veggie garden there right now and plant what is appropriate to the season.
- Stock up on oils, dried noodles, condiments and pasta. Put dates on everything so you can slowly rotate your stock.
- Take out library books on native edible plants and mushrooms and go for walks so you can learn to identify them.
- Form groups with people around you for learning and teaching skills.
- Take your local farmers to lunch. Support them and love them because you might need them one day. Wait — that's shallow. Just support them and love them!
- If you begin to learn to live without the fancy things now, it will be easier to slip into a different life later. And this way is so much easier on the planet.
- Be nice to your planet and maybe it won't kick you in the bum.

- Buy canning jars and lids to have around for when you need them.
- Call friends to see who can give you canning lessons.
- Look for spaces in your home where you could store extra food.
- Clear these areas out, wash the shelves and get them ready for stocking up.
- Think of two people who preserve and store food and phone them and ask to visit them for ideas.
- Put a few sheets of paper on the fridge with a magnet and write down items you should buy or have on hand, as you think of them.
- Look in your phone book for the nearest plant nursery, and write on your calendar when to visit them and buy vegetable seeds.
- Buy or clean an existing plastic tote for food storage.

And with an extra hour a week:
- Work on a list for an earthquake kit.
- Plan a shopping day to begin your stash.
- Walk through your garden and mentally block off the spaces where you'll be planting more food plants.
- Spend a half hour a week clearing and preparing the garden for planting.

Resources

Cyber-Help for Organic Farmers, certifiedorganic.bc.ca/rcbtoa/ training/organic-seeds.htm.

This site lists organic seed houses in BC, GMO free!! But the Cyber-Help site itself has many links to farmers and farms and is jam packed with help for market gardeners as well as those growing large scale.

This chapter was written with love to all my co-workers.

CHAPTER 15

Working Cooperatively

Modern humans feel pretty smug, with all our great appliances, cybersmarts and investigative science. But we are losing one important facet of life very quickly — the ability to share well and freely. Anthropologists are fairly certain that when ancient people brought a big hunk of dead animal home, they didn't just drag it into their cave and slam the door. They shared it. There was probably some nasty pecking order involved, with Uncle Bob getting prime rib and Jimmy getting the feet and tail, but hoarding food for oneself seems to have come along later in the game. We also seem to have come a long way, backwards, when it comes to sharing tasks. Getting together to haul in a fishing boat at the end of the day or make the baskets for the big rice haul have not quite translated to the North American mall scene. Some of us know we have to change this, but certain aspects of sharing can feel frightening at first. We may be afraid that we will do all the giving, and nothing may come back. Or we may feel that someone we are sharing with could exploit us in some way, leaving us feeling stupid and vulnerable. These are protective thoughts and keep us safe, but learning to share is a good skill to have, especially if we are on our own, elderly, a shut-in, or otherwise a bit vulnerable. Sharing opens the world up like a big jar of homemade jam — new experiences, opportunities and adventures all have a chance to be tasted and savored. We can learn to share on our own time, slowly and carefully at first, then getting more and more confident that we are still safe, and are now part of a thriving community where we can truly step out and make change.

Here are some things that can be shared:

Knowledge: Do you know how to dry herbs, fix a wheelbarrow tire, bake bread or make jam? Can you make wine, save seeds or grow healthy seedlings? Fix a heater or repair a greenhouse? These assets are very important to share.

Tools: Saws, pole pruners, an air pump for somebody's deflated wheelbarrow.... If you see a need, make an offer of your tools. Just paint them bright pink and they will always come back to you, or offer to do the fixing yourself.

Space: We take space for granted, but maybe there is room in your crawlspace or back porch for people to store their winter food or earthquake kit. Perhaps you have a shady spot in your garden that someone with Sierra desert conditions needs for their cool crops.

Time: It's such a priceless commodity! Looking after a couple's toddler so they can get their garden in, picking up books for someone working too long to get to the library — time is a great gift and if we think hard, we can usually see where it would do the most good.

A healthy body: Next time you think you need an hour at the gym, please consider whether all your local seniors have their potatoes in, firewood stacked, and apples picked.

Motor vehicles: Those without cars have trouble taking advantage of sales of bulk items, or lugging a bag of seaweed home. Since they're already doing us a good turn by using fewer fossil fuels, we could surely take them along when we run our big errands. And don't wait for them to ask — you know who needs you.

Freezer space: A full freezer uses less electricity than a half-full one. Is there someone local who would benefit from a little space so they could stock up on deals from the supermarket?

Love and caring: Asking a co-worker what is wrong, and then listening, taking a moment to touch someone on the arm if they are stressed out, offering to help with that eyesore of a broken fence instead of silent blaming. Our own lives get more precious when we take time to share bits of portable love.

On Being Dragged Into Community

I tell my friends I am a hermit, and they laugh their heads off. I do suppose that being surrounded by rabid, highly social gardener-type friends does make it difficult to separate myself back out of the matrix. What do you do with a gang of giddy folk who feel the world is abundant and that everything must be shared? Kick them out? Tell them to stay home? No matter how hard I try to be a grouchy loner, I keep spotting someone heading up my driveway with a suspicious bag under his or her arm.

The Sunshine Coast is still pretty isolated. When they unplug the ferry at night, we are all trapped here together, doing the best we can with the community we live in. I'd say we do a damn good job. My home is in Roberts Creek, where many of the best lunatic garden nuts live, and I think we have reached a pinnacle of material and not-so-material wealth juggling. Tools, potato tubers, seeds and canning jars make a jagged but tenacious path from home to home. Skills and knowledge float overtop of that in a hazy circle, dropping gently onto unsuspecting people when they really need it.

My cupboards contain Erin's jam and Alain's garlic. Janet's carrot salad is almost used up in my fridge. Maria, who does my income tax, threw in two free buckets of chicken manure. Harry, Adrian and Judy have all donated apple trees. Val is going to teach me how to pressure can some halibut on the weekend and Robert is coming over to help me weed. How is a woman supposed to stay reclusive in a town like this? Arggh! The horror!

And as my garden assets have bred themselves into insane abundance, I have been more and more able to throw a few things of my own into the mix. Surely, I can part with a few strawberry plants. Do I really need fifty-seven raspberry bushes? I am slowly prying my worried fingers off of the little green gems and pushing them into the world, and as I do so, to my surprise, some quantum type thing happens where it all multiplies and flings itself out one-hundred fold. Those plants grow other plants, and those get given away, and so on.

Of course, I don't want this to soften me up. This sharing and caring stuff gets a bit heady on a hot day. You almost have to hide behind the curtains to keep from getting free stuff on you. Oh wait. I think that's Janet coming up the driveway with some beans. Gotta go.

Sharing Shapes and Forms

At its smallest, sharing starts with one person who perceives a problem and feels like diving in to fix it. I have a memory of standing at my kitchen window in town years ago, watching the rain fill the streets with water. The drains on the streets were clogged with leaves and many figures crowded windows that day, watching the water rise over the lawns. Then mid-afternoon, when it seemed that the water would reach the surrounding homes, I saw a wet, hooded figure move down the road. He was carrying a rake and stopping at each drain to rake mittfuls of leaves up and away from the metal grates, till the water flowed down, and then he headed down to the next one. The water slowly seeped away, and we all moved from our windows, more than one of us, I hope, saying, "A-ha — so that's how it works, one human just deciding to fix it. A-ha."

And sharing of work or things can take place between any co-operative people. Two folks putting in a compost bin, chopping a tub of rhubarb, picking the apples, pressure canning the last of the soup — companionship and a place to trade information as well as a way to get the job done. Naturally, this situation is ideal when the two parties have slightly different abilities, so that a dovetailing effect occurs, but no sense quibbling over tiny details when there's a job to be done.

We had something up here on the Sunshine Coast we used to call the SWAP team, where four of us rotated between each house on Sunday mornings, doing whatever the resident there wished for two hours. We cleaned tool and gumboot covered porches down to the bare wood, and re-organized the results into boxes and piles. We dug weeds out of rhubarb patches and planted garlic. We placed mulch and fixed fences. Nothing ever seemed to take more than two hours. We were lucky when we went to Robert's house, because he would serve rich dark coffee and warm muffins, and equally happy when Maria pulled out the home made bread and soup. Things slipped badly at my place (apples and tea — I am still learning to cook), but the gracious workers never said a thing. It got harder and harder for us to pull the Sundays together and we gradually let it slip, but I still look at certain areas of my garden and remember that a single morning pulled it together. I swear there are still warm energy shapes hovering out there.

Naturally, as with all combinations of matter, these teams work better when a lot of diversity is displayed. We needed Robert's long arms and strong back, and we needed to have the tenacity, lateral thinking and organizational skills represented by the others to pull our work off quickly. We needed to be open to other people's approaches and to the fact that the vision we had in our heads may not be what we ended up with.

On a larger scale, it has been discovered that barn raisings and sewing bees still work! Inviting the more capable and enthusiastic among your friends to help with a single project can be fun. Putting raised beds in a backyard, building a community root cellar, getting a greenhouse up or putting storage shelves in a basement goes a lot faster with skilled hands. Don't forget to have food, bevies, and music if possible. If you are short on party treats, just invite as many kids and dogs as you can. That always improves the ambience.

If you are still trying to find cooperative souls, there are many clubs and societies in every community. However, just because there are eighteen people in a room who like to garden doesn't mean they are going to end up bosom buddies. It takes a while to discover the people who have the same crazy notions as yourself, so be patient when you join a group, and let the personalities play out before you start the "will you be my friend" thing. And sheesh, why does the "will you be my friend" thing raise so many eyebrows? Every four-year-old knows that it's the perfect question to ask, and we should all still be asking it.

Learning from Sentient Beings

When the folks at Momentum Magazine suggested the prefix "co" as in "cooperation" as a theme for an upcoming issue, I swung my old wooden chair around and looked out into my garden. Most of my best lessons come from there. The more species of weird and wonderful, strange and magical plants that I throw in there, the more luxuriant and powerfully they all seem to grow. That must mean they hold the secret to this cooperation thing.

I pull on my boots and head out to see what I can learn. First, I spot a big clump of the still standing French sorrel. The man from Columbia who brings garden teachings to us up here had pointed out on his last visit that sorrel's ability to stay green through a drought was of more benefit than just to it-self — it was able to exude this humidity around it in a small cloud, where nearby plants would benefit. Other plants that stayed fresh looking through the summer dry spell were notice-able for being near the sorrel plants in my garden. I pluck and nibble on a leaf tip as I head around to the driveway. There I see a somewhat lonely yarrow colony planted in a newly emptied mound. I recall that this had been the three-year long home of a small apple tree, snapped off by an equally small horse at its last home and given to me in case it could be saved. Well, I was dubious. I planted it, pulled the dying top upright, and wrapped the open stem fracture in electrical tape (there be-ing no duct tape at hand). I then planted yarrow around its base and mulched them both well. One of my books spoke of yarrow as a "nurse plant" that pulled hard to find nutrients and other plant medicines from deep down, releasing them around its own base. A human might wonder at the benefit of giving away all that goodness, but yarrow plants never have wars, so we may have to sit back and consider our ways.

At any rate, the apple tree had leafed out that first spring after it was moved in, and looked almost normal. The second spring, it pushed out some flowers. The third year, it produced a single apple near its very slender top. This apple grew in size and bent the tree over until the tip hung low to the ground. I watched this from a distracted distance, until I noticed the leaves dying, and on closer inspection saw that the weight of this single progeny had pulled the weak old piece of electrical tape away, permitting the unclosed fracture to yawn wide once again. The tree soon died and I gently pulled it out and laid it in the bush, apple intact. Did that yarrow give the tree the three years it needed to complete its task? I now feel a surge of guilt at not planting the apple seeds, and move on down the garden.

The chives under the other fruit trees seem to be doing a good job of keeping nasty bugs from being attracted to their stems. And not a single strawberry in the medicinal garden had been browsed by deer. I wonder if the spot plantings of strong tasting feverfew, purple sage and vervain are driving them away. It works for me, and it works for the strawberries as well. I pass the winter garden where the chickweed is cooling the soil under the collard greens and purple sprouting broccoli. When this dies down, it will provide a protective mulch as well as a nutritious slow release feed in the spring. That's what annual plants do — they die down and feed the soil so that it can support their offspring for another year — the last big gift. We keep pulling these so-called weeds away, but we're crazy. Chickweed for instance has a NPK ratio of 77-34-220. Compare this with cow manure at 11-3-9. Go there. Our weeds are hyperloaded food supplies and they keep the soil rich with their death.

I walk past the fence that is woven with the unpruned vines of grape, honeysuckle and tayberry. I suppose I should be clipping and shaping these each year, yet they seem to fold around each other,

From Hermit to Community Member: A Primer

- Start at the beginning. Next time you wonder if you should lend your best gardening book to the new guy at work...well, you probably should.
- Start at the back. Begin your giving with that senior down the street who won't remember who you are. The people next door who you're trying to impress can wait.
- Practice is a very good thing.
- Say "yes" whenever possible.
- Remember that if "war" is someone wanting all the power/oil/land for themselves, then "peace" must be the state of wanting others to share in what we have. Live your belief.
- Remember that if everyone in your community had equal access to food and skills, there would be fewer bogeymen out in the night wanting your stuff.
- Don't worry about running out of assets if you give them away. Some weird thing is going on out there. You will still have enough.
- Don't forget that time is a sharable asset.
- Ideas and emotional support are renewable resources and cannot ever be all used up.
- Remember that community begins exactly and precisely where you are sitting right now.
- Receive from others happily and enthusiastically.

producing abundant quantities of fruit and flower without my messing about, so I imagine they know what they are doing and are making room for the survival of all. Certainly, some plants suffer. Late germinators sit stunted for months under an overpowering, slightly older sibling. Although if I remove that larger plant, the little one has merely been waiting for its chance and will re-grow quite normally when the opportunity arises. It has been crouching in the shade and humidity of someone who is better able to cope with the sun's raging power. There is no rush.

I stand back in the gathering autumn rain, near a pile of greenery growing brown for winter, shedding its bounty of nutrients onto all who surround it, food for the worms, food for the microorganisms — food for all. In the spring, they will slowly reawaken, push each other gently out of the way, and proceed with their task of oozing nutrients and moisture and medicine into the world around them, ceaselessly and without diminishment. This is the lesson I can take back into my human world with me.

CHAPTER 16

Choosing Your Future and Feeling Your Big Muscles

At a certain point in our food security awareness, we start tracing back a very strange food chain and begin to see where we fit into it. And we discover a funny truth: We are at the bottom of our food chain. Many choices are apparently offered to us in our grocery stores — a wealth of them in fact — at least, we are offered what the corporate chains wish to make available to us, on their terms. But unless we buy organic foods, we can't choose to eat food that is not irradiated, and we cannot tell if food has GMOs in it because our government refuses our petitions to have that information available. We can't buy local food at the supermarket because it does not fit in with their shipping systems. We can't even decide to support food grown in our country, because the label will say where the food was packaged, but not where the contents came from. It is now illegal for us to buy a chicken from a farmer down the street who cannot afford to take this animal to an abattoir — so the doors of the small farm gate food sales are being banged shut by our governing bodies just as our awareness for need opens up. True food security gets harder to access as the global economy becomes more powerful and unbalanced.

It's going to take a long time to wrest power over our food supply back into our own hands, but it feels imperative to more and more of us that we begin to do this. We have become very dependent on a system that no longer feels compelled to support the consumers' wishes and needs, and it is time to turn this boat around. We, as communities, certainly do have to make our needs felt by our local grocers, and we need to vote with our dollars and support which foodstuffs we purchase and which ones gather dust. We need to examine our buying habits and see which unwieldy monster we are feeding with our little paychecks. There is so much in our grocery carts we don't actually need in order to survive, and there is so much our small growers could be providing us. As well as pulling our dollars out of the conventional system, we have to begin creating alternatives as near to ourselves as we can. We need to find people around us who would be eager to grow us food, we need to help them use high intensity growing methods, and we need to support them so they can achieve this. We have to make healthy local food a priority in our lives, more important than our need for status, or our need for amusement. Priorities have gotten all wonky in the past decades and we would all be a lot healthier if we got back on the trail.

A major issue in bringing about large change is the perception that individuals are powerless against big business — that our gestures are too small. Well, guess what. No gesture is too small. Heaped one upon another, these gestures are building momentum and are beginning to show up on the landscape.

We outnumber our policy makers. We have to start pulling our cash back out of their pockets and imagining the world we want, and then using our dollars and muscles and brains to make a new shape. We need more local growers, no matter how small. We need to glean food out of our gardens and public spaces. We need food markets and bicycle delivery systems and a new way of eating that does not include faraway sources that we have no control over. Small symbiotic systems have worked through the past centuries, and this is a good time to fit them, as well and as fast as we can, into our future.

Resources

MacKinnon, James and Alisa Smith. *The 100 Mile Diet — A Year of Local Eating*. Random House Canada, 2007.

This young couple took the plunge and spent a full year gleaning what they could from a given area. It was not easy, but their experience was intriguing, and the 100 Mile Diet is now a recognized term for turning back to your own environment for sustenance.

Moore, Richard. *Escaping the Matrix: How We the People can change the world*. The Cyberjournal Project, 2005.

This book explains the much bigger global picture, how we are affected by it, and provides insights into the mental steps that we as individual humans can take to begin changing the power structure of our political world.

Tracey, David. *Guerrilla Gardening: A Manualfesto*. New Society Publishers, 2007.

From the global back down to the local, the people and the projects they choose that are making a difference in their own communities are documented here with love and respect. Lots of ideas for making small scale change right on your street.

CHAPTER 17

Pulling It All Together

Whether it's being too broke to buy a good meal, sitting out an unexpected snowstorm, or waiting out a human-created calamity like a trucking strike, many of us will have to face restricted access to food at some point in our lives. As we know, having our safe, familiar world pulled out of shape can cause distress to body and mind. Being prepared and capable allows us to push through trouble with a smaller amount of real distress, to recover faster from short-term emergencies, and to adapt to permanent change more readily.

Our culture is loaded down with fear as it is, encouraged, as we are to buy more insurance, get home alarm systems and to be afraid of strangers, fraud, and funny looking emails. The wild advantage to being food-secure is that it will actually make our world a better, safer place. More people buying locally, means fewer dirty trucks on our overloaded roads, and more small farmers getting encouragement and support so that they can take risks and increase capacity. Buying organically translates to fewer pesticides not only in our bodies, but in the bees and butterflies, creeks and rivers as well. Buying in bulk and knowing how to store food reduces trips to the store — and fewer car trips means less fossil fuel used, as well as having more time to do good things in our world. If we have lots of food put away we can look after ourselves in a fix and the attention of emergency crews can be directed to those who absolutely cannot help themselves. Our own independence makes us more capable of giving to and helping others. Being food secure means we have skills that we can pass on, creating a tighter community that is not afraid to give rather than take. Being food secure creates understanding and respect for the energy it takes to fill our bodies with energy and nutrients, and this helps to decrease the tons of waste food in our society, and less wasted food means thousands fewer acres being slashed and cleared for stuff that will get scraped down the garburator. Being food secure means having a bond with the miraculous stuff that fills our bodies and regenerates our cells, making us new again.

Much about home based food security is about adding new bits all the time to our personal system until we feel we can sleep well at night. Steps might feel small at first but can be crucially important. Laying that first groundwork of knowledge gathering and thinking, putting that first case of soup away, having a local farmer hand us a sack of earth-scented potatoes, or putting that first home canned jar of peaches on the shelf — these all lead to bigger steps.

Learning to shop before the cupboards are bare so there is always plenty of overlap, knowing what to do in an emergency and learning how to glean the most from a food garden are long lasting techniques we can use anywhere, anytime, and can only benefit the bigger systems that affect us and the planet.

Creating Short- and Long-Term Goals for Food Security in Your House

Many of the Dieticians of Canada use a food security continuum designed by Laura Kalina, but there are other models out there. I like this model because we can take it and bring it down to household size. Here's the broad model used by dieticians and some food security councils to help bring security to communities.

Stage 1: Short-Term Relief

These actions provide immediate and temporary relief to hunger and food issues. These activities are often completed with little or no involvement from those experiencing food insecurity. (Examples: Food banks, soup kitchens.)

Stage 2: Capacity Building

These actions are often more costly in terms of time and manpower and require commitment from those experiencing food insecurity, but are steps to empowering those experiencing food insecurity. (Examples: community kitchens, community gardens, food buying clubs.)

Stage 3: Redesign

Redesign actions are broader in scope and require a long-term commitment from representatives of the entire food system, including in particular, those marginalized by the system. As such, redesign actions are often the most costly, time consuming and difficult to mobilize communities to pursue. Redesign actions focus on addressing problems thought to be underlying food security. This is often thought of as working "upstream" to create system change. (Examples: food policy, social advocacy to address poverty.)

These strategies are all great and our government is working hard to make these work. These "stages" made me wonder how the householder could convert them for use, depending on whether they were looking at income shortfalls or preparing for a rainy day. Based on the food security model developed by governments, here are a few stages I developed with the householder in mind.

Stage 1: Short-Term Relief

Find local growers and know where the local food bank is, find others to form a bulk-buying club, assess personal priorities on spending, track down local soup kitchens, be aware of sales, begin storing access food.

Stage 2: Capacity Building

Analyse weak spots (resistance, too tired), increase learning skills by networking and joining library, seek out growing space, work out prearranged goals with growers, beginning of garden space, read about food growing and canning.

Stage 3: Redesign

Push your government to support local farms, press designers to put food gardens and food storage areas into houses and apartments, make sure that your town has farmers markets several times a week (and support them!) and pressure your health department to either do a better job of educating or to relax regulations that continue to strangle small ventures. Press your government to back off on the meat regulations that make buying local meats illegal.

Creating a personal Stage Two and Three would lead to a world where we always have food put by, can access garden space, canning equipment or freezer space, that we have trusting relationships with several nearby growers, that we are secure in techniques for food storage, recognize and use high quality low cost foods and we know how to cook them.

There. Being "redesigned" means that you are now in a position to guide others and to share tips and equipment. Your actions have had the ripple affect of creating dialog, making your mentor more aware of his or her own skills, and a farmer more confident of sales. You will accidentally reduce fossil fuel use, reduce cash flow to unscrupulous corporate agents, and give yourself more quality time to reconnect with family, friends and the earth.

This food security stuff could be catching. That's my hope.

Index

About the Author

ROBIN WHEELER teaches traditional skills, sustenance gardening and medicinals at Edible Landscapes (ediblelandscapes.ca), a nursery and teaching garden in Roberts Creek, B.C. She founded the One Straw Society, a local organic growers group.

She started the Sustainable Living Arts School to teach traditional skills such as canning, seed saving and winter gardening. Robin has taught classes including sustenance gardening and herb tea workshops, and has written numerous articles about the politics of food. She spent several years on her local Advisory Planning Commission and was active in securing food security funds and designing programs for these funds in her community. She is also the author of *Gardening for the Faint of Heart*.

About the Illustrator

BERNIE LYON'S illustrations focus affectionately on the little details of human behavior. She is also the illustrator of Robin Wheeler's previous book, *Gardening for the Faint of Heart*. More of Bernie's drawings can be seen at www.BernieLyon.ca

If you have enjoyed *Food Security for the Faint of Heart*,
you might also enjoy other

BOOKS TO BUILD A NEW SOCIETY

Our books provide positive solutions for people who want to
make a difference. We specialize in:

Sustainable Living • Ecological Design and Planning
Natural Building & Appropriate Technology
Environment and Justice • Conscientious Commerce
Progressive Leadership • Resistance and Community
Educational and Parenting Resources

New Society Publishers

ENVIRONMENTAL BENEFITS STATEMENT

New Society Publishers has chosen to produce this book on recycled
paper made with 100% post consumer waste, processed chlorine
free, and old growth free.
For every 5,000 books printed, New Society saves the following
resources:[1]

20	Trees
1,772	Pounds of Solid Waste
1,949	Gallons of Water
2,543	Kilowatt Hours of Electricity
3,221	Pounds of Greenhouse Gases
14	Pounds of HAPs, VOCs, and AOX Combined
5	Cubic Yards of Landfill Space

[1]Environmental benefits are calculated based on research done by the Environmental
Defense Fund and other members of the Paper Task Force who study the environmental impacts of the paper industry.

For a full list of NSP's titles, please call 1-800-567-6772 *or check out
our web site at:* **www.newsociety.com**

NEW SOCIETY PUBLISHERS